Rockwell Kent, "Moby Dick"/The Chase: Second Day",
Courtesy Plattsburgh State Art Museum, SUNY, NY

DEAN SCAROS

REFLECTIONS *ON* A
SIMPLE TWIST OF FATE

Literature, Art, and Parkinson's Disease

Scripture taken from the King James Version of the Bible.

ISBN: 978-1-4834-6925-6 (sc)
ISBN: 978-1-4834-6926-3 (hc)
ISBN: 978-1-4834-6924-9 (e)

Library of Congress Control Number: 2017907354

Lulu Publishing Services rev. date: 06/15/2018

For Emily and Alexander

Contents

Author's Note

I originally intended this book to be read primarily by people who, like me, are living with Parkinson's disease. My plan was to make it available exclusively in the waiting room of the Neurological Institute of Columbia Presbyterian Hospital in New York alongside the usual literary assortment found in such places. As the book began to take shape, however, it became apparent to me that the issues I was writing about were not unique to those of us with Parkinson's. They applied in equal measure and with equal urgency to almost anyone afflicted with a life-threatening illness. Faced with traumatic diagnoses, human beings, it seems, confront the same demons and angels.

Therefore, the structure of the book reflects my original intention of making it available in a medical waiting room. Chapters have been kept short and self-contained, and liberal use is made of illustrations to enhance the text so that whole sections can be read in a short time. And since the book is organized as a compendium rather than a sequential narrative, the chapters need not be read in tandem.

The title page of each chapter includes a copy of a painting or photograph accompanied by selected prose or poetry. The painting and the literary selection relate to the subject of the chapter but not necessarily directly to each other. They are each meant to be thought-provoking in their own right. I hope that the reader will derive as much value from these selections as from the text itself.

Preface

The compensation of growing old, Peter Walsh thought, coming out of Regent's Park and holding his hat in his hand, was simply this; that the passions remain as strong as ever, but one has gained—at last!—the power which adds the supreme flavour to existence—the power of taking hold of experience, of turning it round, slowly, in the light.

—Virginia Woolf, *Mrs. Dalloway*[1]

On the waiting room wall of the Columbia University Neurological Institute's Department of Movement Disorders in New York City, there once hung a painting created by a person with Parkinson's disease, an upstate business owner. Nearby was a collection of his poetry. The painting, which was titled "Frozen Face," was designated as a self-portrait of the artist, his face wrapped mummy-like in a rust-colored winding cloth. As a pair of startled eyes peer through the shroud, the effect is macabre, but to anyone with Parkinson's, the reference is clear. Parkinson's eventually causes rigidity of the facial muscles, which can lead to a permanently expressionless face, a condition known as "masking." Thus, some people with Parkinson's can't smile. They endure the irony of losing to their illness a faculty that might otherwise help to mitigate its effects.

The painter of "Frozen Face" is expressing one aspect of his struggle with the disease. Contained in those haunting, thunderstruck eyes is the bewilderment many of us feel when suddenly faced with serious illness. My chance encounter with that painting led to the writing of this book.

While I am obliged to that businessman who unknowingly encouraged my own creative efforts, this book takes a very different approach than his project. More about that in a moment. First, it's important to make clear what this book is *not* about.

This is not a chronicle of personal struggle, although my own experience with Parkinson's naturally informs what I've written. Nor does it deliberately aim to be inspirational, though I hope parts of it will inspire. The book offers no direct advice but advice can certainly be inferred from it. And while it invokes the Bible as it does other works of literature, its voice is agnostic and secular. Least of all is this book a how-to guide for coping with Parkinson's disease or a quick read for *"dummies"* looking for a primer on the subject. There is no survey of relevant medical research here, no personal memoir, and no advocacy.

This book has a different purpose. It is to consider through the lens of great literature and art issues that are important to us as we try to come to terms with progressive, debilitating illness. These issues are not physical or clinical (we have doctors for those). Rather they concern the ways in which we think and feel about our experience and how we choose to deal with it.

Understandably, such an approach might prompt the question, "What does literature or art have to do with Parkinson's disease or any other illness?" The answer is … nothing and everything.

On the one hand, no illness, least of all Parkinson's disease, is an abstraction. Being ill is all too concrete, immediate, and disruptive. In *Illness as Metaphor*, Susan Sontag warns against viewing illness as representing something other than itself. "… the most truthful way of regarding illness—and the healthiest way of being ill—is one most purified of, most resistant to, metaphoric thinking."[2]

There is a relentless physical immediacy to being chronically ill. Many illnesses—especially Parkinson's—never let you forget they're there. There is a certain impudence to their persistence. And most of us are all too familiar with the limitations of medical science. Science gets you just so far, and in the area of neurological diseases, it is rarely far enough. In neurology drugs are largely palliative rather than curative, and they often exact a heavy price in other aspects of our well-being. But despite the gravitational pull of the disease itself, most of us manage from time to time to turn our attention away from its physicality and try to come to terms intellectually and spiritually with what is happening. We then discover that we are not alone.

All of the issues we face have been expressed with great artistic sensibility and insight, affording us the opportunity to better understand and gain a measure of wisdom about our experience. The discussions of literature and art in this book are not *academic*. The works being cited were not chosen because they qualify as some sort of wisdom literature, although the reader will find a decided bias toward the classics, which have had much to teach and illuminate. They were selected because they seem relevant, beautiful, provocative, and in some ways, helpful. They are touched upon lightly and only for the purpose of illuminating aspects of living with serious illness.

Great art and literature are always subversive. They shed light on life's darker corners and transform us in subtle ways. We do not learn from reading literature or looking at a painting the way we learn from other experiences. Rather we are affected in the same way that we are affected by our environment or our families—profoundly but imperceptibly. After a teenager reads Salinger's *The Catcher in the Rye*, for example, the chances are that he or she is altered by the experience in significant but not necessarily obvious ways. Something about Holden Caulfield, something he did or said in that space between the written page and the human mind, touched that teenager's sense of self and changed it forever. This book is meant to be subversive. Its method of provocation is to draw upon some of the best of what has been thought and written and examine our current circumstances through that prism.

"Chinese Horse", Prehistoric Cave Painting, Lascaux Cave,
Courtesy Art Resource, NY

The search for meaning through artistic expression has always been a fundamental and uniquely human impulse. The astonishing cave drawings of Lascaux, Chauvet, and Altamira testify with great eloquence to the human instinct for symbol-making and our age-old search for understanding through creative experience.

Myth-making, too, was an early means by which human beings made sense of things. There is no culture on earth that has failed to construct a mythology, and themes and narratives often exhibit startling similarities across cultures. As Joseph Campbell observed, "When I began to read American Indian myths, I found the same motifs there that I was being taught by the nuns in school—creation, death and resurrection, ascension to heaven, virgin births."[3]

Consider as one case in point a parallel view regarding divinely inspired prophecy held by two very different cultures, namely that of ancient Greece and the *"barbaric"* Celtic world to its north.

According to ancient Greek myth, Zeus released two eagles, one from the east and one from the west. They came together at Delphi, which was then declared the "omphalos," the center of the universe and the threshold to the world of the gods. For hundreds of years, the ancients consulted the oracle at Delphi on matters as mundane as marital squabbles and as momentous as war and peace. For them, Delphi was the gateway to a higher plane of understanding.

An analogous mythic portal found expression in Celtic mythology. In Celtic myth there exists the notion of "thin places." Thin places are "where the visible and the invisible world come into their closest proximity. To seek such places is the vocation of the wise and the good, and those who discover them find the clearest communication between the temporal and the eternal"[4] The oracle at Delphi was such a place, as are Stonehenge and countless churches, temples, and sacred sites throughout the world.

Harvard theologian and Bible scholar Reverend Peter Gomes suggests that thin places are not limited to shrines. They may also include experience. In particular, illness may bring us closer to such places. "Perhaps," Gomes suggests, "we can adapt the concept of thin places to the experience people might have as they encounter suffering, joy and mystery, and seek in some fashion to make sense of that encounter."[5]

As we live with serious illness, we may be in that thin place the Celts imagined where experience is intensified and we are closer to illumination. Emily Dickinson, who may or may not have known of Celtic myths, nonetheless sensed the possibility of a brightening even as a light dims.

> By a departing light
> We see acuter, quite,
> Than by a wick that stays.
> There's something in the flight
> That clarifies the sight
> And decks the rays.

> —Emily Dickinson, *"By a departing light"*[6]

This book is an invitation for those living with Parkinson's and other life-altering illnesses to *reflect* on what is happening to us. Parkinson's often takes words away by impairing our cognitive function. This book attempts to take some back. Through reflection and the liberating power of art, we can make better sense of our encounter with illness and gain a greater measure of solace and even happiness. And—to paraphrase a celebrated literary critic who himself faced a serious disease—through reflection we might keep ourselves from "falling out of our lives into our illness."[7]

Dean Scaros
Ridgefield, CT
Summer 2018

CHAPTER 1

Why Me?

"Abraham and Isaac", Engraving for Bible, CCI The Archive at Art Resource, NY

Tyger, Tyger burning bright,
In the forests of the night:
What immortal hand or eye,
Dare frame thy fearful symmetry?

—William Blake, *The Tyger*[1]

When faced with misfortune, a person might well ask, "Why me?"

A person of faith does so with the presumption that there is an answer but understands that it may not be forthcoming. Atheists, too, ask the question, even though they know full well no divinely inspired explanation exists. In both cases the question is asked rhetorically more as a lament than a real query. To the faithful, God's ways are inscrutable, His judgment infallible, and His voice silent. The answer simply lies in God's plan, which we cannot know. To those who do not believe in a divine being, the universe has no voice or thought or intention. There is no plan.

But those of us whose faith is less certain or whose disbelief is less absolute also ask the same question, "Why me?" We get the same answer—silence.

Unless we are satisfied with the indefinite explanations of science, we mostly find that the answer is simply that there is no answer. Each year 2 percent of the population develops Parkinson's disease. Yet it is also the case that each year nearly 100 percent of the population develops *something*. Many will experience kidney failure. Hundreds of thousands will find they have cancer. Millions will discover a harmless rash, and a few will be struck by lightning.

Although the facts might seem to point to an indifferent universe, we are human after all, and our nature is to regard ourselves as existing at its epicenter. When things happen, they seem to happen *to* us, and if they're happening to us, there is an element of intention about it. And if what happens is illness or catastrophe, we readily imagine a malevolent force as the source of that intention. In *Lord Jim*, Joseph Conrad's novel of a sea captain caught up in the consequences of a moment of moral weakness, Conrad captures the notion that there is something indefinable that has an evil hand in our destiny.

> Only once in all that time [Jim] had again the glimpse of
> the earnestness in the anger of the sea. That truth is not
> so often made apparent as people might think. There are
> many shades in the danger of adventures and gales, and
> it is only now and then that there appears on the face of

facts a sinister violence of intention—that indefinable something which forces it upon the mind and the heart of a man that this complication of accidents or these elemental furies are coming at him with a purpose of malice, with a strength beyond control, with an unbridled cruelty that means to tear out of him his hope and his fear, the pain of his fatigue and his longing for rest: which means to smash, to destroy, to annihilate all he had seen, known, loved, enjoyed, hated; all that is priceless and necessary— the sunshine, the memories, the future—which means to sweep the whole precious world utterly away from his sight by the simple and appalling act of taking his life.

—Joseph Conrad, *Lord Jim*[2]

The truth may be, of course, that no such malevolent force exists and that it is only the natural self-centeredness of human beings that leads us to imagine otherwise. In the absence of such a force or controlling entity willing to explain itself to us, a reasonable conclusion is that no die has been cast, no destiny fulfilled, no justice served by our particular circumstance. We are afflicted because we *are*. There is no clear logic for what befalls us. There is only the fact of it. "Time and chance happeneth to [us] all."[3]

Nonetheless, Conrad seems to feel otherwise. He echoes the book of Job in its affirmation not only of the existence of evil but of its active intentions as well. Early on in the book of Job, there is a convocation of God's minions very much like a king holding court. Satan is in attendance and has this remarkable exchange with God.

Now there was a day when the sons of God came to present themselves before the Lord, and Satan came also among them. And the Lord said unto Satan, Whence comest thou? Then Satan answered the Lord, and said, "From going to and fro in the earth, and from walking up and down on it."[4]

There is something spectacularly ironic if not comedic in the image of Satan simply wandering about the earth as if he were on a Sunday morning stroll, considering the magnitude of the havoc he wreaks on mankind. The exchange between God and Satan turns out to have dire consequences for Job, who—very much like each of us—is minding his own business. God asks Satan if in his walking "to and fro" in the world, he has taken note of Job, "a perfect and upright man, one that feareth God and escheweth evil."[5]

Clever dialectician that he is, Satan acknowledges that he has, but faithfulness, he argues, would be expected of one who, like Job, has enjoyed every blessing God could bestow on a man. Satan asserts that misfortune would expose Job's true character and cause him to "curse [God] to his face." God accepts the challenge of finding out (or more accurately, allowing this challenge to move forward), and Job famously becomes the human battleground upon which goodness and piety vie for supremacy over evil and faithlessness.

Job loses everything—family, health, and wealth. God acknowledges that in testing Job with all manner of calamity, he has been moved by Satan against Job "without cause." Thus, if Job is regarded as the archetype of the human condition, we must resign ourselves to the fact that catastrophe will almost certainly come to us sometimes unexpectedly and wholly "without cause." However, like Job who does not waiver in his faith despite enduring unimaginable calamity, we, too, have a miraculous capacity to remain steadfast.

Misfortune visited Abraham differently in the form of a command from God to sacrifice his only son, Isaac. Like Job, Abraham did not ask, "Why me?" He simply packed up and took his son to the designated place in the mountains of Moriah. At the moment he lifted the knife to kill the boy, an angel of God called his name, "Abraham! Abraham!" to which he answered, "Here am I."[6]

"Here am I" is among the most consequential utterances in the Bible. It is first and foremost a declaration of unconditional faith. But even more remarkably, it dramatizes Abraham's spiritual strength as rooted not only in blind faith but in his freely exercised choice to comply. Rather than seek to evade the command by attempting a discussion with God beginning with him saying, "Why me?" he chose to stand his ground, to *be* without question. Abraham's (and Isaac's) salvation comes as the result of Abraham's decision to choose to accept a power greater than himself rather than defy or question it. Abraham's "Here am I" stands in sharp contrast to the reaction of Adam, who, after eating the apple offered by Eve, heard God call his name and hid from His sight.[7]

Christ Himself exhibited weakness analogous to that of Adam when in Gethsemane He pleaded, "If it be possible let this cup pass from my hand." There was no answer. This moment of recoiling in fear—so universal a human reaction—was also expressed earlier in the Old Testament in the Psalm 22 of David.

> My God, my God, why have you abandoned me?
> Why so far from my call for help, from my cries of anguish?
> My God, I call by day, but you do not answer; by night,
> but I have no relief.

Ultimately, the psalmist and Christ accepted silence as an answer to the question "Why me?" They acceded to a power beyond human understanding. The same choice presents itself to all of us.

Surely, everyone does not choose alike. Some demand an answer, and in its absence many remain in a constant state of rage or despair. Some seek justice. Others harbor resentment against the forces that have sickened or maimed them, and they can think only of revenge. Such was the case with Melville's famously obsessed captain of the Nantucket whaler *The Pequod* and his doomed quest.

CHAPTER 2

Defiance or Acceptance

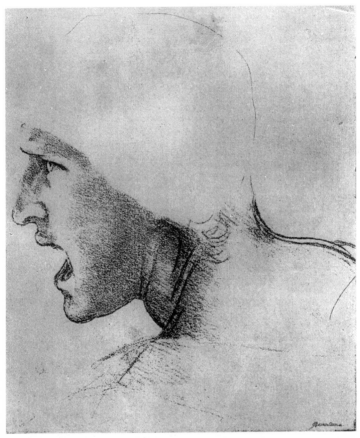

Leonardo DaVinci, "Drawing of Shouting Warrior",
Foto Marburg/Art Resource, NY

"A dead whale or a stove boat!"

—Herman Melville, *Moby-Dick*[1]

With the notable exception of Milton's *Paradise Lost*, there is no greater narrative of rage and defiance written in the English language than Herman Melville's *Moby-Dick*. The story is simple. A whaling ship captain known to us as Ahab loses a leg to a notorious white whale called Moby-Dick and becomes obsessed with hunting it down and destroying it. He sets sail from Nantucket in command of the newly provisioned whaler, *The Pequod,* and a full crew that includes Ishmael, a young sailor and the narrator of the tale. While Ishmael senses a certain pall over Ahab and the upcoming journey, no one save Ahab himself is aware of the mission he has in mind for the *Pequod.*

Soon, however, Ahab's boundless rage and determination to exact revenge become clear to the crew. Starbuck, the first mate who is repelled by the notion of a blood feud with what is essentially a force of nature, protests, "Vengeance on a dumb brute!" He exclaims, "That simply smote thee from blindest instinct! Madness! To be enraged with a dumb thing, Captain Ahab, seems blasphemous."

Ahab's response—mad though it may be—gives voice to man's primal instinct to defy and destroy the forces that threaten him whether they be natural or divine.

> All visible objects, man, are but as pasteboard masks. But in each event—in the living act, the undoubted deed—there, some unknown but still reasoning thing puts forth the mouldings of its features from behind the unreasoning mask. If man will strike, strike through the mask! How can the prisoner reach outside except by thrusting through the wall? To me, the white whale is the wall to me; I see him in outrageous strength, with an inscrutable malice sinewing it. That inscrutable thing is chiefly what I hate; and be the white whale agent, or be

7

the white whale principal, I will wreak that hate upon him. Talk not to me of blasphemy, man; I'd strike the sun if it insulted me.[2]

For those of us afflicted, Parkinson's disease is our great white whale—indifferent, unstoppable, inscrutable, and inexplicable. Whether it has risen to smite us from the depths as the result of some malicious or divine design or just because of dumb luck is of no consequence. We are "{dismasted" by it just the same.

We have a choice to make. Do we become Ahab?

In making such a choice, our will is not entirely free. We are not the product of our own invention. Our choices—even those that seem very personal—are colored by our culture. Some cultures, for example, have evolved to protect tradition, to be wary of change, and to revere the past with a bias toward fatalism and acceptance of one's lot in life. Other cultures encourage change and innovation and promote the independence and rights of the individual over the group. In the West—and particularly in America—our habit of mind is to envision things as they ought to be rather than as they are, and defiance rather than submission is regarded as the nobler choice. Above all, we strive for and *expect* mastery over the natural world, and that includes the diseases that afflict us.

These patterns are written in history. Among the great ancient civilizations, most were insular and inward-oriented. Egypt worshipped death and so expended its energy and resources to build fantastic tombs for its pharaohs and nobility. China developed extraordinary cultural refinement over five hundred millennia only to contain it behind great walls. But in the West, Plato convinced us of the existence of universal laws, of absolute perfection and our intellectual capacity to conceive of it if not to attain it. Alexander led an army from the Ionian Sea to the Hindu Kush. Sailing ships from Lisbon circumnavigated the earth. Marco Polo pried open the court of Kubla Kahn. In the Western mind, all things are possible.

In this cultural environment, why then should Ahab's inclination *not* be to strike against the leviathan until "he spouts black blood and rolls fin out"? Likewise, why can't we *"conquer"* space and reach the moon and *"eradicate"* poverty and terror and injustice? And why can't we *"defeat"* Parkinson's?

Our culture's overarching *sine qua non* for success is not luck, magic, privilege, or caste but *struggle*. Our historic strength has been in challenging what *is*. And this also is our great weakness. Ahab, after all, met his death on the very day he planned to triumph in his drive to avenge his loss and to "strike the sun." The rope of the harpoon he had thrust into the white whale's flank became tangled around his neck, and as the whale dove again into the depths, he dragged Ahab to his doom.

When we insist on explanations of the inexplicable or resist the irresistible or refuse to accept what *is*, we risk nurturing in ourselves the rage of Ahab ... and his fate. We nourish demons like disappointment, embarrassment, resentment, and fear. And like Ahab, we risk exhausting our energies and turning our soul into a haunted place.

This is certainly not an argument against defying long odds. It is important to recognize, though, that offering resistance is on the opposite side of the spectrum from another alternative we might consider. As one spiritual teacher put it, when things fall apart, we might do well to ask of ourselves, "Am I going to practice peace or am I going to war?"[3]

> Ah, when to the heart of man
> Was it ever less than a treason
> To go with the drift of things,
> To yield with grace to reason,
> And bow and accept the end
> Of a love or a season?

> —Robert Frost, from *Reluctance*[4]

It does not seem to be in our nature, as Robert Frost makes clear so simply and beautifully, to "go with the drift of things." It is a kind of treason against our nobler selves. We tend to associate resistance with courage and acceptance with defeat, and our language and culture strongly reinforce this bias. This country was born of revolution. We admire the defenders of the Alamo for fighting to the last man and mottos such as "Live free or die," "Give me liberty or give me death," and "No surrender" are deeply embedded in our cultural psyche. Irish poet Dylan Thomas famously exhorted us all to "Rage, rage against the dying of the light." Milton's Satan, the fallen angel and real hero of *Paradise Lost*, announces the same choice with steely defiance, "And, in my choice/Better to reign in Hell than serve in heaven."[5]

Accommodation, *appeasement*, and *compromise* have become pejoratives. Within such a linguistic context, a degenerative illness like Parkinson's disease is naturally experienced as an *attack* on our neurological apparatus. In response we must *fight* it. Medicine must *eradicate* it.

Alan Watts, one of the twentieth century's most innovative philosophers of theology, characterized the consequences of a *resistance mind-set* as "human beings suffering and perishing from their very attempts to save themselves."[6]

The language and metaphors we use for a disease, Susan Sontag argues, heavily influence and mostly constrain our ability to deal with it. "As long as a particular disease is treated as an evil, invincible predator, not just a disease, most people with cancer will indeed be demoralized by learning what disease they have. The solution is hardly to stop telling cancer patients the truth, but to rectify the conception of the disease, to de-mythicize it."[7]

Those of us with Parkinson's disease might ask, "Is there an acceptable alternative to *declaring war* against it? Is the choice really as stark as heroic resistance or abject surrender?"

Pema Chodron, author of *When Things Fall Apart: Heart Advice for Difficult Times*, argues that *acceptance* and *accommodation* are not a form of resignation but one of enlightenment. She writes, "Things falling apart is a kind of testing and also a kind of healing. We think that the point is to pass the test or to overcome the problem, but the truth is, that things don't really get solved ... The healing comes from letting there be room ... for grief, for misery, for joy."[8]

This point might sound harsh upon first encountering it, but here is what I think Chodron means. Our lives are the aggregate of all our moments. If we strive to deny the moment—even the ugly, difficult, or painful moment—we risk avoiding our lives, imperfect as they may have become.

There is another way to be. Acceptance of Parkinson's or any illness as something that simply is a part of us to be experienced and accommodated allows for our remaining energies to turn elsewhere, to imagine things that have nothing to do with illness, or to leave room for life separate from it. Otherwise, we are imprisoned within our misfortune.

Chodron relates the story of a couple in a small Chinese village deeply grieved by the crippling of their only son as a result of a fall from a horse. Since the young man was an important source of financial support and prestige, they were devastated by this misfortune. Soon after the incident, however, an army came through the village and forcefully conscripted all of its healthy, young men. Their son was spared and stayed behind to help the family survive.

"Life is like that," writes Chodron. "We don't know anything. We call something bad; we call it good. But we really don't know."[9]

The wisdom of acceptance is echoed by Joseph Campbell.

> Is anything in your life that did not occur by chance? This is a matter of being able to accept chance ... Chance, or what might seem to be chance, is the means through which life is realized. The problem is not to blame or explain but to handle the life that arises.
>
> —Joseph Campbell, *The Power of Myth*[10]

Ahab could not accept his misfortune as a stroke of chance. Chance suggests the absence of malice, which Ahab could not imagine. He needed to ascribe his severed leg to a malevolent force that deliberately and unjustly "dismasted" him and turned a "dumb brute," as Starbuck called it, into a mythic figure. Ahab would not rest until he struck back. In doing so, he brought about his own destruction.

CHAPTER 3

Losses and Gains

Arturo Faldi, "Study of a Landscape", Scala/Art Resource, NY

There was a time when meadow, grove, and stream,
The earth, and every common sight
To me did seem
Apparelled in celestial light,
The glory and freshness of a dream.
It is not now as it hath been of yore—

Turn whereso'er I may,
By night or day,
The things which I have seen I now can see no more.

—William Wordsworth, from *Ode: Intimations of*
Immortality on Recollections of Childhood[1]

The passing of time, the peeling away of capabilities that we may have taken for granted over a lifetime take their toll on our spirit and state of mind. The losses experienced by people with progressive and increasingly debilitating illness are more than physical. Personal identity built over long years of work and achievement, social networks, marriages, and friends are all made vulnerable. Some of us may be more resilient than others, but there's never any point to displaying false cheeriness. It's almost always short-lived and "the going up is often not worth the coming down."[2] Likewise, there's no point to despairing. It's how we come undone.

Like other neurological disorders, Parkinson's disease does not do its damage all at once but in small increments. Progression might be slow or swift, and medications can mask some symptoms. But the truth is that Parkinson's disease's special form of havoc is to burden us in two ways—in the actuality of loss and in the certainty of more to come. Psychologically, it's a double whammy.

The losses imposed by Parkinson's are devastating and include jobs, marriages, friendships, and personal independence and mobility. And yet we all know that human beings have an almost limitless capacity for living with great adversity and achieving great things. But the battle-cry metaphor, which is implicit in words such as *overcome* or *conquer* or *defeat*, can obscure other ways of experiencing our condition that involve positive potentialities.

Is it possible, for example, that great things are achieved *because* of great losses? Did Homer's blindness impel him to create? If he had not been blind, is it not plausible that he might have been content to tend a farm somewhere and leave the world to make do without *The Iliad* and *The Odyssey*? Didn't Lear have to lose everything in order to gain something of real value? And was time spent in a stifling Birmingham jail really just the occasion for the writing of Dr. King's "Letter," or was it the creative force behind it?

For these men (Lear's experience being no less illuminating for being fictional) losses were matched by gains. Loss of sight, loss of kingly power and possessions, and loss of freedom all happened, but these gave way to a more enlightened and inspired state. First comes the wrenching loss so severe that the mind threatens to explode in a primal scream of fear much like Edvard Munch imagines in his haunting vision:

Edvard Munch, "The Scream", Album/Art Resource, NY

Such raw, elemental, and complete suffering, according to Aeschylus, may well be the only means to illumination, and it was also a staple of ancient Greek tragedy.

> Justice so moves that those only learn
> Who suffer: and the future
> You shall know when it is come; before then,
> Forget it.

It is grief too soon given.
All will become clear in the next dawn's sunlight.

—Aeschylus, *Agamemnon*[3]

There is an especially intriguing case to be made for a possible causal link between mental illness (particularly with respect to clinical depression) and creativity. The list of *bona fide* bipolar or clinically depressed artists and writers, for example, is astonishing. A small sampling includes Botticelli, Poe, Picasso, Hemingway, Fitzgerald, O'Keeffe, Plath, Tolstoy, Matisse, Munch, and countless others. The list is long. And yet for all the research that's been done, the matter remains inconclusive and largely in the realm of speculation. One report from Texas A&M University evaluated and assessed twenty-nine studies and thirty-four review articles on creativity and mental illness, and researchers found that of the twenty-nine studies, fifteen found no evidence linking mental illness and creativity. Nine found positive evidence, and five had unclear findings. Interestingly, among the studies examined was one that selected forty-three American published poets and compared them to a random sample of the general population measuring the incidence of clinical depression among both groups. No significant differences were evident.[4]

The study of the link between physical as opposed to mental illness and creativity has received comparatively little attention from researchers. That's not surprising since physical illnesses are infinitely more numerous and varied among the population than clinical depression or bipolar disorder. With what physical illness would we start?

Nonetheless, examples of creative intensity coinciding with serious physical illness can be drawn up, and the register is as long and dramatic as that for clinical depression. Michaelangelo, Monet, Toulouse-Lautrec, Montaigne, Goya, Degas, van Gough, Dostoevsky, and Voltaire all suffered from serious illnesses or disabilities. Such instances and countless others fuel the notion of illness as a creative force. Social researcher Tobi Zausner of the New School for Social Research comes to the following conclusion: "There appears to be a connection between illness and creativity in some individuals. Evidence suggests that it is not only the illness, but a person's response to the illness, that leads to a new stage of life and new work. Even though a physical ailment can be debilitating, certain individuals have also found it to be motivating."[5]

The point here is not "Gee, aren't we lucky that we've got a serious health problem so now we can all write novels." Rather the idea is that gains often accompany losses. The gains might even be a direct result of the losses and often turn out to be of greater value. Whether by causality or coincidence, at least the circumstantial evidence is substantial.

Accordingly, serious illness need not be all about losses but of gains as well. We know little about the physiology of the mind. Perhaps at the onset and progression of Parkinson's and other neurological disorders, something occurs in the brain's neurological pathways that affects the imagination. Perhaps in the course of disruption and molecular chaos, new avenues of thought are opened. Maybe in the wall we see before us, there is a doorway.[6]

In exploring the relationship between creative energy and illness, the lives of the Romantic poets of the nineteenth century are exemplary. They lived with chronic infirmities and pointedly drew inspiration from them as if they were wellsprings. In the process they dealt with themes of great relevance to us—the nature of time, loss and memory, and the consolations to be found in the simplicity and beauty of the natural world.

The greatest of the Romanic poets were either always ill or imagined they were. William Wordsworth suffered from debilitating migraines, amnesia, and frequent chest, flank, and arm pain, and he was tormented by an obsessive dread of blindness. John Keats developed tuberculosis and died at twenty-six. Lord George Gordon Byron endured a painful clubbed foot. He suffered declining health in his prime and died at thirty-six. Samuel Coleridge endured gout, scrofula, epilepsy, and rheumatic fever and was addicted to opium. And Percy Bysshe Shelley was a model of ill health and crippling hypochondria. He was subject to nervous attacks, addicted to laudanum (an opium and alcohol *medicinal*) and was suicidal.

Nonetheless, in what might be characterized as a magnificent irony, the Romantic poets embraced *nature* as their source of inspiration and enlightenment. The very force that was causing them such great physical distress (and as we've seen curdled into maniacal rage in Melville's Ahab) fired their imagination and produced poetry that—at its best—is sublime and a balm for the human spirit.

As people living with Parkinson's, we are acutely aware of the passage of time. Our illness is time-bound, and we think of it in those terms: when it wasn't, when it was, what it is now, and what it will be. Yet demarcating our lives into segments that are characterized by degrees of loss, we may be making it harder to see our actual selves in full. "To live life, and not death-in-life, gently yet forcefully Wordsworth advises us to find the natural continuities between what we were and what we are."[7] Our bodies age; we evolve.

Wordsworth's beautiful "Ode" laments the loss of innocence when as children everything seemed to us "appareled in celestial light/The glory and freshness of a dream." The years pass. We gain experience and suffer loss, and the seemingly idyllic world that we entered as infants "trailing clouds of glory" steadily recedes in memory. In its place—to the degree that we allow it—comes the harsher and more cynical sensibility of adulthood, which distances us from ourselves and the natural world that had been such a source of wonderment.[8] But in our hearts there remain enough threads of the child's skein to weave together joys of a different kind.

> What though the radiance which was once so bright
> Be now forever taken from my sight,
> Though nothing can bring back the hour
> Of splendour in the grass, of glory in the flower;
> We will grieve not, rather find
> Strength in what remains behind;
> In the primal sympathy
> Which having been must ever be;
> In the soothing thoughts that spring

Out of human suffering;
In the faith that looks through death,

In years that bring the philosophic mind.[9]

For Wordsworth and for us (if we allow it), the philosophic mind is not about philosophy at all but about our willingness to come to terms with our experience. The philosophic mind is the solace we can find in the petals of a rose, in our memory of more innocent and less encumbered days, and in our imagination, which can yet give us the capacity for "thoughts that do often lie too deep for tears."[10, 11]

CHAPTER 4

Courage

"The Last Stand at the Alamo", Pennsylvania Historical Society,
Art Resource, NY

Neither the countenance of a threatening tyrant, nor Auster, the ruler of the stormy Adriatic, nor the mighty hand of thunder-hurling Jupiter can shake his firm soul.

—Horace, *Odes*[1]

Courage is among our highest values. Archetypes from Herakles to Siddhartha to Beowulf and King Arthur to John Glenn and Neal Armstrong have embedded in our cultural sensibility a very clear idea of what is noble in human behavior and what is not.

It is generally acknowledged that there are three types of courage. *Physical* courage can be defined as the quality of behaving fearlessly in the face of possible or certain annihilation. Leonidas at Thermopylae, Washington at Valley Forge, Pickett's charge at Gettysburg, Sergeant York in the Argonne, Audie Murphy at Holtzwihr are but a small sampling of the narratives we carry with us. *Moral* courage is displayed by those who follow the dictates of their conscience without regard to the censure of others, while *intellectual* courage is the quality of accepting and acting upon inconvenient truths. Moral and intellectual courage seem less spectacular and dramatic than physical courage but no less venerated. Socrates drank hemlock rather than kowtow to his accusers. Martin Luther King, Jr., sacrificed his life for principle. Nelson Mandela never broke faith with his cause.

Jacques Louis David, "The Death of Socrates", Princeton University Art Museum/Art Resource, NY

21

> I do not know what affect my accusers have had upon you, gentlemen, but for my own part I was almost carried away by them—their arguments were so convincing. On the other hand, scarcely a word of what they said was true.
>
> —Plato, *Socrates' Defense (Apology)*[2]

Socrates spoke those words in the presence of his accusers and with the certainty that he would be sentenced to death both for his alleged crimes as well as his defiance of the established authorities.

Perhaps no other experience in life presents us with the challenge of acting with courage than the onset of a life-threatening illness. Immediately, before being informed of the diagnosis—feigning ease and relaxation in a waiting room—we might even hear the sound of distant thunder. Suddenly, words spoken by our physician—simple and familiar words like "Good morning. Please have a seat" or "I've reviewed your results with Dr. So-and-So" or "We think your prognosis is encouraging"—words that never in the past carried a hint of menace now drop like stones at our feet. We may react by being startled or crushed or stoical, but the fact remains that we have been pushed into another life without our permission. And some illnesses with their uniquely unpleasant assortment of infirmities might even require firmer stuff from us than might be the case with less debilitating diseases.

In most Western societies and certainly among Americans, the pressure is great to *bite the bullet* and carry on as unflinchingly as possible. The cultural rulebook tells us (as sometimes does our own conscience) that we should avoid becoming *a burden to our loved ones*, emotionally and otherwise. The expectation is to display quiet courage, the kind devoid of the glory of slaying a hundred-headed Hydra or charging into a hail of bullets in defense of a nation. There is no denying, too, that in our culture gender further complicates the issue. A special sanction is reserved for men who do not meet adversity with grace. There is hardly a greater disgrace than cowardice under fire.

Ernest Hemingway, among our most influential architects of what constitutes physical courage, expresses it with characteristic clarity. His is a stoical and almost welcome confrontation with danger and death. Facing their inevitability with unblinking resignation marks the courageous man from the coward. In the closing moments of *For Whom the Bell Tolls*, Hemingway's Robert Jordan sacrifices his life for a cause and in defense of his comrades and lover. In order to buy time for them to escape, he lies in wait on the forest floor for the approaching enemy and certain death. Into a single line of exquisitely understated language—the last line of the novel—Hemingway compresses his view of life, self, and death. "He could feel his heart beating against the pine needle floor of the forest."[3]

We are always alone with ourselves and our choices. At some point life will end for all of us, if not heroically, then in midthought or midsentence or in a darkening haze without fanfare and with only the feel of our heart beating. Whatever meaning our life had, we ourselves gave it ... or failed to give it. It would not have been an accident but an act of volition that we met adversity with grace or renewed purpose or generosity. It is our choice to be steadfast or to yield.

Of course, the subject at hand being life and literature, there is always an "on the other hand." And so, on the other hand, why should we feel bound by proscriptive ideas of what an appropriate response is to mortal danger or serious illness? Why must we be bound by conventional notions of *quiet courage* when that might not be our *natural* reaction? We might be needy. We might be frightened. Why pretend otherwise? If there is comfort in railing against our predicament, complaining about our condition, or cursing the Fates, we ought to be free to do so. Is this cowardice or catharsis?

Like so many other issues involved in the complex business of coping with illness, there is no definitive answer. Yet there is one yardstick that might be regarded as near to objective as possible. It is the yardstick of efficacy. Does the behavior we display regarding our condition actually *work* for us? Is it productive, or does it promote healing? Does it connect us with others, and is it reciprocated with what we require for sustenance, especially compassion, dignity, and respect ?

When first I encountered *Macbeth* as a young student, I was struck by the powerful figure of Lady Macbeth and the cold-blooded purposefulness of her ambition. Despite her evil intent, she is an admirable and even seductive figure. Through the character of Lady Macbeth, Shakespeare obliterates any assumptions we might have had about the limits of female courage and ruthlessness, and in the process he illuminates a critical distinction between courage and cowardice.

Macbeth had earlier committed himself to killing Duncan, the king of Scotland, in his drive to usurp the throne. But now he wavers. Enraged, Lady Macbeth reminds him of his oath and urges him to steel himself for the task at hand.

> Lady M: I have given suck, and know
> How tender 'tis to love the babe that milks me;
> I would, while it was smiling in my face,
> Have pluck'd my nipple from his boneless gums
> And dash'd the brains out, had I so sworn as you
> Had done to this.
> Macbeth: If we should fail?
> Lady M: We fail?
> But screw your courage to the sticking place,
> And we'll not fail.

> —William Shakespeare, *Macbeth*[4]

And what, after all, is a "sticking place?" *The Oxford English Dictionary* defines it as "the place in which a thing stops and holds fast," and specifically with reference to Macbeth, "… the screwing up of the peg of a musical instrument until it becomes tightly fixed in the hole." Macbeth's wavering is unacceptable to Lady Macbeth. She is convinced that courage can assure success and it is success that is of paramount importance not whether the act is good or evil. Vacillation and cowardice lead only to failure. If we can muster the courage to hold fast, we give ourselves the best chance for the best outcome. If we don't, things can get wobbly. They don't work.

Macbeth's last-minute show of cowardice was due to his falling into despair that the plot he and Lady Macbeth were pursuing would fail. He seemed to be making the mistake of believing that courage is the absence of despair. Macbeth misses the point, but we should not. As the psychoanalyst Rollo May observed, "Courage is not the absence of despair; it is the capacity to move ahead *in spite of despair.*"[5]

CHAPTER 5

Dignity

Honore Daumier, "Don Quixote", BpK, Berlin/Art Resource, NY

Commending himself with all is heart to his Lady Dulcinea ... and well-protected by his shield, with his lance in its socket, he charged at Rocinante's full gallop and attacked the first mill he came to; and as he thrust his lance into the sail, the wind moved it with so much force that it broke the lance into pieces and picked up the horse and knight, who then dropped to the ground and were badly battered. "Didn't I tell your grace," [said Sancho Panza] "to watch what you were doing, that these were nothing but windmills ?" "Be quiet, Sancho my friend," replied Don Quixote. "Matters of war, more than any others, are subject to continual change."

—Miguel de Cervantes, *Don Quixote*[1]

In our culture as in many others, there exists a primal bias against illness and old age that is difficult to shed. Our prehistoric ancestors, living each day on the edge of survival, must have taken a dim view of unproductive mouths to feed. That bias has remained in our psychic chemistry. And when illness and old age both converge in one individual, it can prompt the kind of resentment expressed by Michel de Montaigne, the great French essayist, in his famously bitter remark about his own condition, "Nature should have been content to make old age wretched without making it ridiculous as well."[2]

Parkinson's disease is a notorious offender. Often it takes from us qualities that are closely associated with dignity, most notably steadiness and grace. We shake. Our stride is halting. Our voice is soft. Our posture is stooped. Language and metaphor intensify the loss. We speak of a dependable person as being "steady as a rock." We instinctively listen more attentively to a *commanding*, *strong*, or *stentorian* voice. We define elegant bearing as *ramrod straight* and characterized by fluidity of motion and gesture. In the place of a steady hand and graceful stride, Parkinson's leaves us with their polar opposites, tremulousness and rigidity. Language exacerbates the perception of indignity—the weak *waver*, the ineffectual *stumble*, uncertain voices *quiver*.

In such a context, people living with Parkinson's might regard their struggle to maintain dignity as quixotic, tilting at windmills. Yet there is nobility in tilting at windmills.

In the world's first and perhaps greatest novel, Cervantes presents us with the gift of Don Quixote, self-appointed knight errant. Riding an old nag named Rocinante, accompanied by a bumbling Sancho Panza as his *squire*, and in defense of the honor of the incomparably beautiful Dona Dulcinea de Teboso (in whose radiant presence no other beauty may be praised), Don Quixote sets out to right the wrongs of the world. Can there be a more futile or foolish enterprise than that? Can there be a less likely man to pursue it than a gaunt, aging, and slightly addled Senor Quexana of La Mancha? Has any man cut a more undignified figure than that of Don Quixote astride Rocinante?

Don Quixote is an immense novel—at once simple and complex, and in some instances beyond interpretation. It is timeless. It asserts with a power no other novel has approached the inexhaustibility of human dignity and the certainty of the existence of the *good*. Outward appearances notwithstanding, Don Quixote is the archetypal hero disguised as the fool, the better to captivate us with the truth. When he is denounced as a fraud by a cleric in the court of a nameless duke and duchess, Don Quixote speaks of his quest,

> I, influenced by my star, follow the path of knight errantry, and because I profess it I despise wealth but not honor. I have redressed grievances, righted wrongs, punished insolence, vanquished giants, and trampled monsters ... I always direct my intentions to virtuous ends, which are to do good to all and evil to none; if the man who understands this, and acts on this, and desires this deserves to be called a fool, then your highnesses, most excellent Duke and Duchess, should say so.
>
> —Miguel de Cervantes, *Don Quixote*[3]

Through the character of this ragamuffin and seemingly delusional old man, Cervantes assures us that human dignity is not about the steadiness of our hands or the grace of our stride but the generosity and goodness of our intentions and the constancy of our hearts.

"One thing you don't have a choice about right now—and we're working on it—is that you have Parkinson's," Michael J. Fox has said. "You don't have a choice about that. But around that nonchoice, there are thousands of other choices that you still have. You're still intact. You're not 'You minus that.' You're not defined by that. So that means you can go out and be a bad golfer if you want. It's okay to be shaky. You can be shaky and still be steady." Don Quixote was very shaky … and very steady.

As for the irrelevance of outward appearances in measuring dignity, we need not look further than Muhammed Ali. It is a surpassing irony that he among all of us was afflicted by Parkinson's disease. In his prime he was the world's finest athlete, a champion possessing incomparable gifts of power, speed, and grace. That was all lost. But his personal dignity remained intact to the end, hard-won by his achievements and the constancy of his good intentions in the service of his faith and principles.

It does not seem necessary to be a Muhammed Ali to retain one's dignity in the awkward and chaotic physicality of Parkinson's. One could simply be an old gentleman from La Mancha. Human dignity is not defined by tilting at windmills or diminished by the frailties of illness.

CHAPTER 6

Enchantment

"Marc Chagall, "Memory of the Magic Flute" Scala/Art Resource, NY

In Xanadu did <u>Kubla Khan</u>
A stately pleasure-dome decree:
Where <u>Alph,</u> the sacred river, ran
Through caverns measureless to man
Down to a sunless sea.
So twice five miles of fertile ground
With walls and towers were girdled round:
And there were gardens bright with sinuous <u>rills,</u>
Where blossomed many an incense-bearing tree;
And here were forests ancient as the hills,
Enfolding sunny spots of greenery.

But oh! That deep romantic chasm which slanted
Down the green hill athwart a cedarn cover!
　A savage place! As holy and enchanted
By woman wailing for her lover!
　　And from this chasm, with ceaseless turmoil seething.
　As if this earth in fast tick pants were breathing
　A mighty fountain momently was forced:
Amid whose swift half-intermittent burst
Huge fragments vaulted like rebounding hail,
Or chaffy grain beneath the thresher's flail:
And mid these dancing rocks at once and ever
It flung up momently the sacred river.
Five miles meandering with a mazy motion
Through wood and dale the sacred river ran,
Then reached the caverns measureless to man,
And sank in tumult to a lifeless ocean:
And mid this tumult Kubla heard from far
Ancestral voices prophesying war!

The shadow of the dome of pleasure
　Floated midway on the waves:
Where was heard the mingled measure
From the mountain and the caves.
It was a miracle of rare device,
A sunny pleasure dome with caves of ice!
　　　A damsel with a dulcimer
　　　In a vision once I saw:
　　　It was an Abyssinian maid,
　　　And on her dulcimer she played,
　　　Singing of Mount Abora.
　　　Could I revive within me
Her symphony and song,
　　　To such a deep delight 'twould win me,
That with music loud and long,
I would build that dome in air
That sunny dome! Those caves of ice!

And all who heard should see them there,
And all should cry, Beware! Beware!
His flashing eyes, his floating hair!
Weave a circle round him thrice,
And close your eyes with holy dread,
For he on honey-dew hath fed,
And drunk the milk of Paradise.

—Samuel Taylor Coleridge, from *Kubla Kahn: A Fragment*[1]

Illness can be overwhelming, and Parkinson's can be especially so. It can become the center of gravity of our lives, a kind of black hole that threatens to pull every conscious moment inward toward itself. The effect is hard to avoid as so much of our lives is touched by our infirmity. And of course, Parkinson's is a showy disease—difficult for others to miss and difficult for us to ignore.

Ironically, one casualty of this persistent reality is *unreality*. As our illness and health concerns command more and more of our attention, we can become consumed by the here and now of coping. In the process we stand to lose our capacity for simple reverie and our ability to be enchanted.

In his extraordinary book *The Re-Enchantment of Everyday Life*, philosopher and theologian Thomas Moore observes, "An enchanted life has many moments when the heart is overwhelmed by beauty and the imagination is electrified … The soul has an absolute, unforgiving need for regular excursions into enchantment."[2]

As children, we were frequently and easily enchanted by new things and fresh imaginings. As adults, we've seen it all … or too much … or enough. Having seen the Great Oz behind the curtain, we've turned into realists (maybe even cynics) and lost sight of the delights of wonder. Perhaps we've allowed ourselves to become too smart or too spiritually exhausted and fail to see that wisdom requires an honest appreciation of mystery.[3]

Creative artists, in particular William Blake, understand the uses of enchantment in man's search for meaning. Blake's mystical, often ambiguous verse and fantastical etchings are designed to fire our imagination and move us closer to illumination.

William Blake, "The Four and Twenty Elders Casting their Crowns before the Divine Throne", Tate, London, Art Resource, NY

For Blake, enchantment lay in the astonishing imagery of his mystical poetry. It seems he believed that the mind contains its own secret revelations, and that the work of the artist is that of a kind of sapper—to cause an imaginative explosion that will generate heat and light in equal measure. His genius was in the creation of stark and provocative imagery and a deep sense of the mystery and wonder of life that he compressed into poems of often sublime beauty.

> Does the eagle know what is in the pit?
> Or wilt thou go ask the Mole;
> Can wisdom be put in a silver rod?
> Or love in a golden bowl?

> —William Blake, "Thel's Motto" from *Songs of Innocence*[4]

In a world that has grown all too real, what is left to enchant us? Are we still capable of wonder, or have our lives devolved into a daily struggle with the tyranny of circumstance?

No one is beyond the reach of wonder but one must be open to it. And once we're in its thrall, it may be best to allow it to be what it is and not attempt to turn it into something that we must decode. Years ago I hired a magician to entertain at my daughter's birthday party. He was a sleight-of-hand artist who could make half-dollars disappear or jump unseen into little pockets and emerge from behind ears. He was flawless. Delighted children begged to see more. But I thought, *How did he do that?* The adult mind strives to pull back the curtain. The children were happy to just let the magic be.

In *Pacific Overtures*, Stephen Sondheim echoes the delight and mystery of life's "small" things and hints, too, that they are what really counts and where we can find a measure of wisdom.

> It's the fragment not the day.
> It's the pebble not the stream.
> It's the ripple not the sea,
> That is happening ..."
> Not the building but the beam,
> Not the garden but the stone.[5]

As children we have all known enchantment, and only the most hardened or unlucky among us has not known it in adulthood. It is everywhere if we are willing to engage it—in music and art, in sports and in play, at dusk and in the early light of dawn, in the chimes of an old clock. It is in the high crown of an oak and the slow spirals of a hawk, in a bonsai pot, in our yard and at the edge of the sea. And it is in a certain slant of light that does *not,* (dear Emily Dickinson), always oppress like cathedral tunes but can turn the gray bark of an old plane tree into silver slate.[6]

And of course, words have enormous power to enchant. They can be the countervailing force to the maelstrom that each day pulls us toward disenchantment if not outright despair. The issue is whether enchantment is even possible for us anymore. Perhaps the weight we carry has finally become too great for flights of fancy. Or if it *is* possible, can it occur in an unlikely place and time—that is, the place you occupy now as you read this?

On either side the river lie
Long fields of barley and of rye,
That clothe the world and meet the sky;
And thro' the field the road runs by
To many-tower'd Camelot;
And up and down the people go,
Gazing where the lilies blow
Round an island there below,
The island of Shalott.

Willows whiten, aspens quiver,
Little breezes dusk and shiver
Thro' the wave that runs for ever
By the island in the river
Flowing down to Camelot.
Four gray walls, and four gray towers,
Overlook a space of flowers,
And the silent isle imbowers
The Lady of Shalott.

—Alfred Lord Tennyson, from *The Lady of Shallot*[7]

Or this, in which the poet is enchanted by a flock of swans?

The trees are in their autumn beauty,
The woodland paths are dry,
Under the October twilight the water
Mirrors a still sky;
Upon the brimming water among the stones
Are nine-and-fifty Swans.

Unwearied still, lover by lover,

They paddle in the cold
Companionable streams or climb the air;
Their hearts have not grown old;
Passion or conquest, wander where they will,
Attend upon them still.

But now they drift on the still water,
Mysterious, beautiful;
Among what rushes will they build,
By what lake's edge or pool
Delight men's eyes when I awake some day
To find they have flown away?

—W. B. Yeats, from *The Wild Swans at Coole*[8]

Or finally, this, a simple coin—a silver obol minted in Athens circa 450 BC? Two obols paid for a mason's labor for a day or for admission to a play at the Theater of Dionysos. Was this coin paid to a laborer working on the Parthenon? Or did it pay for a seat at a performance of *Antigone*?

"Silver Tetradrachm", c. 450 BC, Athens. Private Collection, D. Scaros,

With such an object in hand, it is still possible to find oneself wondering.

For some people—lucky ones, I think—enchantment does not rely on unique objects or events or even people. Life itself is the wonder,

> All my moral and intellectual being is penetrated by an invincible conviction that whatever falls under the dominion of our senses must be in nature and, however exceptional cannot differ in its essence from all the other effects of the visible and tangible world of which we are a self-conscious part. The world of the living contains enough marvels and mysteries as it is—marvels and mysteries acting upon our emotions and intelligence in ways so inexplicable that it would almost justify the conception of life as an enchanted state.
>
> —Joseph Conrad, *The Shadow Line*[9]

CHAPTER 7

Solitude

Edward Hopper, "Nighthawks", Friends of American Art
Collection, 1942.51, The Art Institute of Chicago

No, it is impossible; it is impossible to convey the life-
sensation of any given epoch of one's existence—that which
makes its truth, its meaning—its subtle and penetrating
essence. It is impossible. We live, as we dream—alone...

—Joseph Conrad, *Heart of Darkness*[1]

Illness is a solitary experience. We might have caregivers who bring us
comfort, but the experience is ours alone and cannot be shared. This is not
to say that families and friends are unaffected. Their lives are disrupted,
and long-held bonds may strengthen or weaken under the circumstances.

But illness occupies one body at a time, and if it's ours, we are locked in it alone. We come to know the illness's rhythms and the signature peculiarities of *our case*. It is an unwelcome intimacy but an intimacy nonetheless.

We are not alone in feeling alone. The literature and art of solitude and alienation is vast and has been with us from our beginnings. Far from home and detached from all social connections, Odysseus calls himself "Nobody" when asked his name by the cyclops Polyphemus in his cave. And at that point in his long journey, he *was* nobody. Only when he returned to Ithaca and reclaimed his wife and kingdom was he again Odysseus in the full.

However, not until nearly two thousand years later when Nietszche declared God to be dead in his novel *The Gay Science* (1882) did the notion of personal estrangement begin to be a revolutionary cultural force. With that assertion, Neitszche shook the foundations of traditional society and dislodged the roots of personal identity. If God is dead, then each of us is utterly alone. What's worse, however, is that we are left with Ivan Karamazov's shattering conclusion that if God does not exist, then everything is permitted.[2] Everything can be rationalized. Falsehood is truth, good is bad, bad is good. Everything is moral in the absence of an immovable center.

As the twentieth century unfolded, it did indeed seem as though God had died and everything was permitted. Darkness descended everywhere. Hundreds of millions dead in a pandemic, two world wars, Nazism, communism, fascism, Stalinism, the Holocaust, countless gulags, brutal revolutions, the rapid crumbling of nations and institutions that had stood for centuries—all this seemed to prove Neitzsche right. Could a God worthy of worship possibly exist and abide this horror? Humanity was set adrift in a turbulent and lawless sea. This sense of abandonment and alienation is expressed with searing perfection by the very first line of Albert Camus' novel, *The Stranger* (1942), which reads, "Mother died today. Or maybe it was yesterday, I don't know."[3]

As Parkinson's disease takes its course, some of the qualities that once gave shape to our identity slowly erode. By small increments we take on the mantle of *patient*. In the eyes of the culture at large, if not our own, *patient* is a lesser variant of *person*. Patients are dependent on the ministrations of others. By contrast, persons are independent actors. When among persons, patients understandably feel alone and apart. Anyone who has worn a hospital gown in the company of those fully clothed knows the feeling well.

In the absence of a God to assist us or an Abraham's unequivocal faith to brace us, the only defense against estrangement and alienation is to assume responsibility for ourselves. It requires that we take command of our own lives however difficult that may be and with whatever means have been left to us.

The existentialists—those who reject determinism and believe one can and must create one's own destiny—understood this well. Theirs was a revolt against the threat of a person becoming a *thing* in the wake of an oppressive, impersonal, demeaning, and alienating industrialized society. A chronic, debilitating and progressive illness such as Parkinson's is an analogous threat to maintaining genuine societal engagement. It is precisely because of the reality that we are alone within our illness that we must act in order to give meaning to our lives and get outside of it.

The existentialists' insistence on self-actualization was presaged nearly two hundred centuries earlier. Rabbi Hillel, one of Judaism's great sages and scholars who lived in the time of Herod, declared, "If I am not for myself who is for me? And when I am for myself, what am I? And if not now, when?[4]

As unlikely a dinner group as they would make, Rabbi Hillel and the existentialists (Kierkegaard, Neitszche, Camus, Sartre, Simone de Beauvoir among them) would agree, I think, that the choice of remaining a person rather than becoming a patient is a critical existential decision. In other words, it is an issue that bears directly on the character of our existence. Despite their optimism that one *could* define one's life, the existentialists did not delude themselves into believing that the *desire* to do so would readily lead to it *becoming* so. Yet they made no excuses and consistently counseled action over inaction and hope over resignation.

The existentialists extolled the power of what could be called *creative being*—of really being alive, of making choices and taking control of those things that can reasonably be controlled. The opposite of being, of course, is nonbeing or nothingness. Buffeted by gods and sorceresses, sirens and titans, Odysseus had it exactly right. At the moment he was most out of control and vulnerable in the cyclops's cave, he truly was, as he called himself, "Nobody." But as Odysseus demonstrated, nobodies have the choice of becoming somebodies.

The alternative to creating who we are—the default position not just for those of us with Parkinson's but for anyone in this trackless world—is to allow oneself to remain estranged, a victim of circumstance, adrift and slipping slowly closer to nothingness. In that case we would be indeed be going forth "...you and I/When the evening is spread against the sky/Like a patient etherized upon a table" only to return empty-handed with the lament of the lost and forlorn.

> I grow old ... I grow old ...
> I shall wear the bottoms of my trousers rolled,
> Shall I part my hair behind? Do I dare to eat a
> peach?
> I shall wear flannel trousers, and walk upon
> the beach.
> I have heard the mermaids singing, each to each.
> I do not think that they will sing to me.

—T.S. Eliot, from *The Love Song of J. Alfred Proofrock*[5]

We can be free. But how free can we be?

Jackson Pollock, *"Number 1A"*, The Museum of Modern
Art/Licensed by SCALA/Art Resource, NY

Jackson Pollack's response through *Number 1A* (see previous image) is that we are as free as we insist on being. In *Number 1A*, Pollack seems to suggest the disintegration of conventional forms and of externally imposed order. In their place he creates something utterly new, utterly contemptuous of confinement, and completely his own. Ironically enough, the gossamer lines, crisscrossing pathways, and electric energy of the painting seem to evoke Parkinson's disease itself—a fantastical rendering of a submolecular riot. If we permit ourselves for the moment to imagine that Pollack has inadvertently given us an abstract expression of Parkinson's, we might discern in this riotous canvas the infinite and intricate possibilities of beauty even as things break down.

CHAPTER 8

Is This a Dream?

William Blake, *"Milton's Mysterious Dream"*, The Morgan
Library and Museum and ART Resource, NY

I dreamt that I dwelt in marble halls,With vassals and serfs at my side,
And of all who assembled within those walls,
That I was the hope and the pride. I had riches
too great to count, could boast
Of a high ancestral name;
But I also dreamt, which pleased me most,
That you lov'd me still the same ...
That you lov'd me, you lov'd me still the same.

—James Joyce, "The Bohemian Girl," *The Dubliners*[1]

In book 3 of *The Iliad,* Helen stands on the battlements of the city that her adulterous affair has doomed, King Priam beside her. Amassed on the plain before them are numberless Greek forces facing off against the Trojan defenders. Helen is pointing out to Priam the principal Greek warlords. When Priam asks after a man who looks as though "he must be a king," Helen answers, and in the process she recalls her former life as queen of Sparta, "That man is Atreus' son Agamemnon, lord of empires,/both a mighty king and strong spearman too,/and he used to be my kinsman, whore that I am!/There was a world ... or was it a dream?"[2]

The crushing reality of Helen's here and now—a vast armada arrayed before Troy bent on its destruction because of her infidelity—renders her memory of her prior life ephemeral, far-removed, dreamlike. It is as though her mind cannot reconcile two enormously different realities— Greek queen and adulterous princess of Troy. In her case, the present has such weight and force that the past dissolves as a half-remembered fiction. We all have felt the dreamlike quality of memory. We also know that the phenomenon can work in reverse. A present reality might seem so harsh, fantastical, or unthinkable that we resist it as somehow unreal and find ourselves wondering, *Is this a dream? Is this really happening?*

It is not hard to imagine that many people living with Parkinson's disease have at times experienced the past or the present as if it were a dream. On the one hand, the present reality of Parkinson's may seem so overwhelming and definitive that the memory of earlier times free of the disease takes on the cast of a dream. On the other hand, the reality—perhaps the moment of diagnosis—may sometimes seem so unimaginable or even bizarre that we may feel very much as though we stepped into a bad dream.

Separating the substantial from the ethereal and fact from fancy has been a central concern of Western art and philosophy. There certainly will be no attempt here to trace that history. But for those of us living with Parkinson's, the question of what is real and what is not is unavoidable inasmuch as Parkinson's affects the very faculties we use to comprehend the world and ourselves.

"What is real?" may strike us as a question having a self-evident answer. Common sense says that if we see a chair and can touch it and sit in it, it is decidedly real. For Helen, that army out there on the Trojan plain is as real as it gets. The problem, of course, is that while this may be true, it is also true that nothing is quite what it seems. Our own experience as well as the consensus conclusion after two thousand years of philosophical wrangling is that human beings' perception of what is real—that is, our understanding of what is *really* happening—is at best unreliable and at worst delusional.

Parkinson's is certainly real enough, but what of the context in which we are experiencing it? What of physicians' reports and treatment protocols, the attitudes of spouses, children, friends, and strangers, and expectations for our behavior? How is the perception of our reality affected by them? How is it affected by the media and their presentation of information and public images of Parkinson's? In attempting to come to terms with Parkinson's disease, we are negotiating the concrete reality of what is happening to our bodies and the perceptual reality that is heavily mediated by others. The problem is not just the *fact* of mediation but that its biases are often subtle and undetected by us. They simply suffuse our personal world as naturally and inconspicuously as air. To the extent that this is so, we are living in a reality partly of someone else's making. If we remain unaware of the distinctions, we risk living in someone else's dream.

The idea of a mediated reality and its consequences is made clear in Plato's parable of the cave dwellers. In book 7 of *The Republic*, Plato asks his friend Glaucon to imagine a group of prisoners seated in a cavern with their backs against a wall. The prisoners are immobile, shackled hand and foot, and wearing neck braces so that they cannot turn their heads but must face a wall at a short distance directly across from them. Unseen by the prisoners, above and behind them is a walkway, and behind the walkway and along its entire length is the entrance to the cave. Also above the entrance a fire is burning. As men walk back and forth along the walkway, which has a low wall like the partition in a puppet show, the firelight from behind the men casts shadows on the wall that the prisoners are facing.

Having set the scene, Plato continues,

> Plato [to Glaucon]: ... See also, then, the men carrying past the [low wall of the walkway] implements of all kinds that rise above the wall, and human images and shapes of animals as well, wrought in stone and wood and every material, some of these bearers presumable speaking and others silent.

> Glaucon: A strange image you speak of ... and strange prisoners.

> Plato: Like us. For, to begin with, tell me do you think that these men would have seen anything of themselves or of one another except the shadows cast from the fire on the wall of the cave that fronted them?

> Glaucon: How could they ... if they were compelled to hold their heads unmoved through life?

> Plato: And again, would not the same be true of the objects carried past them?

> Glaucon: Surely.

Plato: If then they were able to talk to one another, do you not think that they would suppose that in naming the things that they saw they were naming the passing objects?

Glaucon: Necessarily.

Plato: And if their prison had an echo from the wall opposite them, when one of the passersby uttered a sound, do you think that they would suppose anything else than the passing shadow to be the speaker?

Glaucon: By Zeus, I do not.

Plato: Then in every way such prisoners would deem reality to be nothing else than the shadows of the artificial objects.

Glaucon: Quite inevitably. [3]

After making the point that we are as prisoners perceiving shadows of the real thing, Plato elaborates on his notion of reality by extending the parable. He proposes that Glaucon consider what would happen if one of the prisoners somehow escapes and ascends to the entrance of the cave. There the prisoner would witness what is *really* happening, recognize that his fellow prisoners are deluding themselves, and return to reveal to them the truth of their situation. Both Plato and Glaucon agree that the prisoner would then surely be killed by his disbelieving fellows. "In the region of the known," Plato concludes, "the last thing to be seen and hardly seen is the idea of good."[4] For Plato, we live like the cave dwellers seeing only the shadows of things and thinking they are real.

Unlike the relativism that characterizes much of contemporary thought, Platonism holds that absolute truth, absolute good, and absolute reality exist, and it is their ideal forms that should govern human affairs. The wise and the good can approach knowledge of these *ideas* or *forms*. In other words, it *is* possible to escape the cave, ascend to the light, and discover the reality behind the shadows. Not all of us can reach this level of enlightenment, however. As many readers know, *The Republic* argues for philosopher kings (Plato was no Jeffersonian democrat) and would turn away poets at the gates of the republic.

The point in recounting Plato's parable of the cave here is to underscore that our perceptual lives are heavily mediated in virtually every respect. An obvious example is the intercession of the electronic media between us and the wider reality of national politics and the world at large. Less obvious is the mediation of others in our perception of our illness, limitations, prospects, and potentialities. It is in the nature of the human condition to find ourselves living in a kind of netherworld, facing a wall upon which figures *seem* to be real and things *seem* to be happening.

But it is important, especially when dealing with such grave matters as Parkinson's disease, to consider in what respects we are seeing shadows rather than the thing itself. Parkinson's is not ethereal. The physicality of the disease is not a shadow, but fear of it may be. The parable of the cave is an echo of Virginia Woolf's remark about taking hold of our experience and turning "it round, slowly, in the light." Woolf, like Plato, understands our perennial challenge is to break free from the chains that hold us in our place and to make our way to the entrance of the cave and into the daylight.

CHAPTER 9

Time

Salvador Dali, *"The Persistence of Memory"*, The Museum of
Modern Art/Licensed by SCALA/Art Resource, NY

Indeed, each man or woman desires a bird. Because this
flock of nightingales is time. Time flutters and fidgets
and hops with these birds...The children, who alone have
the speed to catch birds, have no desire to stop time, For
the children, time moves too slowly already. They rush
from moment to moment, anxious for birthdays and new

years, barely able to wait for the rest of their lives. The elderly desperately wish to halt time, but are much too slow and fatigued to trap any bird. For the elderly, time darts too quickly. They yearn to capture a single minute at the breakfast table drinking tea, or a moment when a grandchild is stuck getting out of her costume, or an afternoon when the winter sun reflects off the snow and floods the music room with light. They must watch time jump and fly beyond reach.

—Alan Lightman, *Einstein's Dreams*[1]

Time is not a friend to those of us living with Parkinson's disease. Time's usual benefactions of healing and of the comforting collecting of memories come to us on fewer and fewer occasions. Parkinson's draws strength from time, while we mark its passing with quiet dread or practiced indifference and with losses slowly heaping.

However, as it turns out, time is not immutable. Nor does it *march* as one metaphor would have it. According to Einstein's theory of special relativity, time slows as a body approaches the speed of light. If we were to travel in a rocket ship at 186,000 miles per second, we would age more slowly, and our Parkinson's would advance less rapidly than if we had remained stationary. In the spirit of a parlor game, we might go further and imagine that if we were to travel faster than the speed of light, time would stop altogether. Parkinson's would be rendered dead in its tracks, the cosmic forces themselves robbing it of its *progressiveness*. Unfortunately, we'd be stymied. According to the laws of physics, traveling faster than light is impossible. Time can be slowed. It can even be bent, but it cannot be stopped. Except in the mind of a poet like John Keats.

When we speak of time, we speak of it in terms of being in or out of our control. We counsel ourselves to "seize the day" or to "be in the moment." We regret "time lost," or we are reassured by "time saved." As people living with Parkinson's disease, we cannot be faulted for fearing the advance of time and on some subconscious level, for wishing it would slow or stop. And in any event, if we could stop time, what would we find?

In his "Ode on a Grecian Urn," Keats reflects upon a wedding procession pictured on an ancient vase that he himself has imagined. Depicted on the vase are the bride and groom, musicians, and guests who are leading a heifer to sacrifice. For Keats, this marble urn, this "foster-child of silence and slow time" has suspended a moment in time for us—a wedding, an archetypal *human* moment—that he enters into and discovers the deep themes of his art and our lives.

The moment depicted on the vase excites his imagination. "What men or gods are these? What maidens loth?/What pipes and timbrels? What wild ecstasy?" Keats reflects upon the groom etched motionless on the marble urn in the act of reaching for his bride.

> Bold lover, never, never canst thou kiss,
> Though winning near the goal—yet, do not grieve;
> She cannot fade, though thou hast not thy bliss,
> For ever wilt thou love, and she be fair.[2]

Time suspended is time forever lived but forever unfulfilled; the consolation of unrequited love is endless desire.

The spell of suspended time remains unbroken in the poem as Keats goes on to imagine nature herself forever green, music forever fresh, and love forever in the flush of passion.

> Ah, happy, happy boughs! That cannot shed
> Your leaves, nor ever bid the spring adieu;
> And, happy melodist, unwearied,
> For ever piping songs for ever new;
> More happy love! More happy, happy love!
> For ever warm and still to be enjoy'd,
> For ever panting, and for ever young.

Yet Keats recognizes that no moment, sublime though it may be, can be contained by us. His work—this poem—is a flight of the imagination. Life intrudes. The urn, representing art, can only with a glimpse of the sublime and the eternal. We are mortal, and our generation like others will come and pass. But the urn remains—as *art* remains—"in the midst of other woe/Than ours, a friend to man." Art overcomes time and speaks to us through the ages and affirms life almost as a benediction.

> Beauty is truth, truth beauty,'—that is all
> Ye know on earth, and all ye need to know.

These are two of the most haunting and enigmatic lines in all of English poetry and among the most debated. There is little consensus among critics regarding them, and it is of no small consequence that T. S. Eliot found these lines to be "meaningless" and a blight on a poem he otherwise found to be beautiful.

I leave Keats's lines and Eliot's opinion to the reader's own interpretation with no additional comments except to point out that the lines are about art and our relationship to it whether we are ill or healthy. Keats seems to be saying that a window upon the eternal—an encounter with immortality—opens through art and its expression of the beautiful and the true.

Of what possible use or solace can this idea be to us? Perhaps as we experience the darker side of mortality, we may naturally be drawn more urgently toward the light. Keats suffered from tuberculosis, and he was twenty-four, a year from death, when he wrote this ode; however, he never stopped reaching for the sublime through his art, not unlike a groom reaching for his bride.

In his way, Keats sensed those thin places of Celtic mythology, those portals in our lives that open to the eternal and the divine. He is telling us that they exist as art—poems and melodies, paintings and sculpted urns. And they are of our own making. Those of us living with Parkinson's who are driven to create art or embrace it are joined in common cause with Keats.

Art, of course, does not always take us where we want to go but where we dread to be. What we glimpse from those thin places may be sublime or may sometimes be horrific.

In his novel *The Road*, Cormac McCarthy explores not the suspension but the *death* of time. Imagining a post-apocalyptic world, McCarthy follows the desperate journey of a father and his young son on a road heading south to the sea, where they hope to find warmth or some sort of relief that is never made entirely clear. The world as we have known it simply no longer exists, its remnants recognizable only in the way a decayed corpse might still vaguely resemble its former self. Most of the few humans we encounter in the novel seem to be a part of the detritus of the landscape and turned monstrously evil.

In *The Road*, the past has been obliterated. The present is a hellish, smoldering dystopia, and there is no future. The father is slowly dying, but he and his son continue the trek to the sea as though it held the promise of salvation. They finally arrive only to find a gray, lifeless ocean and the same steel-gray skies they imagined they had left behind.

McCarthy has written his way to the end of time, to the darkest reaches of the human soul. He has nearly eradicated hope and stripped away everything we know that makes us human, including language, which is sparse and clipped throughout the novel.

All along the way, he has the father flirting with what Camus regarded as the central philosophic question in a meaningless universe—whether or not to commit suicide. (Camus's answer was an emphatic no. Meaninglessness calls for revolt, not extinction.) With one bullet left in his gun, the dying father might, as an act of mercy, take his son with him into oblivion to escape from the certain annihilation of the present. McCarthy has brought us to the end of the road in every way possible way, face-to-face with the end of everything.

And there he finds—we find—the still-burning embers of the human soul. The father dies. The son despairs but resolves to go on. He has always reassured his father that he held "the fire" inside him. Appearing suddenly before the boy is a man, rifle in hand. Friend or foe? Miraculously, the stranger turns out to be a friend. He has a wife and two children, and they've been following the father and son for some time. They are prepared to have the son join their family, and he does.

The novel ends at this point. This is hardly a happy ending since the characters remain in the bleakest of all possible worlds. But we cannot know more. What we do know from McCarthy's *Road* is what we know from Keats's *Ode* and perhaps what many of us know on our own. The astonishing human soul beset by forces of extinction somehow survives, transcending time and bending toward eternity. It is inexplicable.

> Once there were brook trout in the streams in the mountains. You could see them standing in the amber current where the white edges of their fins wimpled softly in the flow. They smelled of moss in your hand. Polished and muscular and torsional. On their backs were vermiculate patterns that were maps of the world in its becoming. Maps and mazes. Of a thing which could not be put back. Not made right again. In the deep glens where they lived all things were older than man and they hummed of mystery.

> —Cormac McCarthy, *The Road*[3]

Each of us must confront the passing of time in his or her own way and *on* our own. Admittedly, we're not always as contemplative about it as Keats or McCarthy. Perhaps the long and the short of it is that those of us living with Parkinson's simply feel a greater sense of urgency than most people. We see time as infinite and finite at the same time. The poet Stanley Kunitz put it this way. "The most poignant of all lyrical tensions stems from the awareness that we are living and dying at once. To embrace such knowledge and yet remain compassionate and whole—that is the consummation of the endeavor of art."[4]

Perhaps the part of us that accepts the cycles of life and death imposed by time and nature will always struggle with that part of us that seeks to touch eternity. It may be what makes us truly human. The great Czech writer and playwright Karel Capek—ironically the man who introduced the word *robot* into the language—dramatizes our psychic conflict in his play *The Makropopulos Affair*. One character complains that even sixty years of life is not nearly enough.

> What can a man do during his sixty years of life? What enjoyment has he? What can he learn? You don't live to get the fruit of the tree you have planted; you'll never learn all the things that mankind has discovered before you; you won't complete your work or leave your example behind you; you'll die without having even lived. A life of three hundred years on the other hand would allow fifty years to be a child and a pupil; fifty years to get to know the world and see all that exists in it; one hundred years to work for the benefit of all; and then, when he has achieved all human experience, another one hundred years to live in wisdom, to rule, to teach, and to set an example. Oh, how valuable human life would be if it lasted three hundred years."

> —Karel Capek, *The Makropoulos Affair*[5]

Another character named Emilia, to whom her alchemist father gave a prolonged life of more than three hundred years, responds by asserting that longevity would make for a more miserable life.

> You cannot go on loving for three hundred years. And you cannot go on hoping, creating, gazing at things for three hundred years. You can't stand it. Everything becomes boring. It's boring to be good and boring to be bad … And when you realize that nothing actually exists … You are so close to everything. You can see some point in everything. For you everything has some value because those few years of yours won't be enough to satisfy your enjoyment … It's disgusting to think how happy you are. And it's simply

due to the ridiculous coincidence that you're going to die soon. You take an apelike interest in everything.[6]

The most productive among us and the happiest seem to me to be those who see time as a precious commodity and recognize that to squander it is to squander in some small way our share of the eternal. Among those of us who might believe that life is too short—as many do—or that it has been foreshortened, I would commend for their consideration the view of Lucius Seneca, the Roman philosopher who wrote in the first century AD,

> Most human beings, Paulinus, complain about the meanness of nature, because we are born for a brief span of life, and because this spell of time that has been given us rushes by so swiftly and rapidly that with very few exceptions life ceases for the rest of us just when we are getting ready for it... It is not that we have a short time to live, but that we waste a lot of it. Life is long enough, and a sufficiently generous amount has been given to us for the highest achievements if it were well invested. But when it is wasted in heedless luxury and spent on no good activity, we are forced at last by death's final constraint to realize that it has passed away before we knew it was passing. So it is: we are not given a short life but we make it short.
>
> —Lucius Seneca, "On the Shortness of Life"[7]

CHAPTER 10

Creativity

Jankel Adler, *"An Abstract Fish"*, The Jewish Museum,
New York/Art Resource, NY

The imperfect is our paradise.
Note that, in this bitterness, delight,
Since the imperfect is so hot in us,
Lies in flawed words and stubborn sounds.

—Wallace Stevens, *The Poems of Our Climate*[1]

Many people living with Parkinson's experience a heightened desire to create after diagnosis, which may or may not be related to the disease. Some have even described their creative activity as a "compulsion", some as "a catharsis," and some as "therapy."[2] I will leave it to social scientists and psychologists to uncover empirical evidence that affirms a causal connection between the onset of Parkinson's and creativity or debunks it. It does not seem to matter either way. No finding is likely to render those who are creating any less eager to do so or any less prolific.

There is in the act of creating a defiance of impermanence and a revolt against silence. Painting a picture, particularly when a stubborn brush finally touches a canvas *just so*, or writing a poem in the dead of night strikes a blow against nothing. Nothing is what is on a blank canvas or a fresh page. And for those living with Parkinson's disease, nothing is a looming presence. We live with the specter of nothing … always. We know exactly what Samuel Beckett meant when in his novel *Malone Dies*, Malone declares, "Nothing is more real than nothing."[3]

It takes courage "to bring something new into being," as Rollo May makes clear in his landmark work on creativity, *The Courage to Create*.[4] It's often been said that courage underlies all other virtues. In order to genuinely love another or to be faithful to a cause, we need to confront the truth of the relationship. Otherwise, it devolves into a charade. Likewise, if one is aiming at creating genuine art, one must confront the truth about the subject of the work and one's relationship to it. Confronting the truth is always the challenge of the artist, but it can be a special challenge to artists who are living with Parkinson's disease and who must face truths that are as unnerving as leaning over an abyss.

May goes on to echo Keats in regards to art as the means by which the artist (and the viewer) "are able to reach beyond our own death."[5] Death is the nothing we all face as human beings and the blank we wish to stamp with a mark of our own. Most of us do not aspire to fame or even modest recognition. Immortality does not require that we appear on center stage.

It is enough to carve our initials on a tree. It is enough for us to know that we've said what we needed to say. It is the silence that is intolerable. It is nothing that we cannot abide.

The process of creativity is considerably easier to define than art, which of course is often (though not always) its objective. Creativity, according to May, "is the encounter of the intensively conscious human being with his or her world."[6] Thus, the act of being creative involves a level of heightened awareness and a powerful "encounter."[7] This is a sometimes painful confrontation between the *creating person* on the one hand and on the other, the material he or she is working with and the intellectual and emotional essence of the thing being created. When we find ourselves immersed in this "encounter," the creative process offers the kind of full engagement we rarely find in other parts of our lives.

This may explain why many Parkinson's patients report an alleviation of their symptoms when they are creating. It may be why many people actually become more prolific after diagnosis than they were before. The creative process is a safe harbor against the storm. Paul Klee, among the great abstract expressionists, suffered in his final years from scleroderma and once remarked during this time of his life, "Never have I drawn so much or so intensely. I create—in order not to cry."[8]

In terms of defining art, which is often the objective of creativity, the matter becomes considerably more complex. At least since Plato, who lived in the fifth century BC, philosophers and scholars, artists, writers and poets, charlatans and rogues all have attempted to define *art* as opposed to whatever is *not* art. It has been an inconclusive exercise. Art is as much a human *event* as it is an object. That event has many facets. It involves the creative person and his or her vision as well as the thing created and the cultural and social context in which it is experienced. And of course, it involves a confrontation between the viewer and the thing created. Given even just these few touch points, the permutations for prescriptive definitions of art are nearly infinite.

People living with Parkinson's have produced an enormous body of creative work that is beautiful, fearless, and moving. More importantly, it expresses the emotional life of a community which has been formed by sheer chance and now finds itself bound by common trials. Several works in particular (although there are many) can be seen as representative of the quality and character of creativity among people with Parkinson's, and the powerful voice they've given to a community whose aspirations and fears they embody. By any reasonable measure, much of the creative work of people living with Parkinson's is not what some might dismiss as *merely* therapeutic, cathartic, or recreational but genuine art.

The portrait on the left is a detail of the painting titled *Juan de Pareja* by Diego Rodriguez de Silva y Velazquez (1650), which hangs in the Metropolitan Museum of Art. The painting on the right, which is called *Frozen Face* by John King (2007), hangs on a wall of a waiting room at Columbia Presbyterian's Neurological Institute.

Diego Rodrigo Velasquez, *"Juan de Pareja"*, The Metropolitan Museum of Art, Art Resource, NY

John King, *"Frozen Face"*, by Permission of the Artist

In the foreword to the museum's own catalogue for a special exhibit of Velasquez's work, the director of the Met, Philippe de Montebello, wrote that Velasquez has a "special place in the pantheon of painters."[9] He went on to affirm Velazquez as being in the first rank of painters. "Velazquez is considered one of the greatest painters of all time—indeed a few years ago I was fascinated to see that he came out first in a London Sunday Times poll of some fifty museum curators, critics, and artists."[10]

What Mr. de Montebello omitted from his comments was that he must not only have been *fascinated* by the *London Times* poll but greatly comforted as well. In 1971, his predecessor, Thomas Hoving, personally approved the purchase of *Juan de Pareja* by the Met for the staggering sum of $5.5 million, the highest price ever paid for a painting at the time. Beside it at the Met is an explanatory gallery label that includes the following:

> [when it was first publicly displayed] the picture gained such universal applause that in the opinion of all the painters of the different nations everything else seemed like painting but this alone like truth. Velázquez manages to convey not only the physical presence of the sitter but his proud character.

> —MMA, gallery label, *Juan de Pareja* by Velazquez[11]

The painting is magnificently executed, and the subject comes alive before us and mesmerizes us with his gaze. As the gallery label points out, Velazquez conveys the character of the subject as well as his physical presence. Juan de Pareja was actually one of Velazquez's slaves, part white and part Moor. There is something astonishing in his regal poise and imperious gaze, which in 1650 must have been seen by the viewer to be in sharp contrast with his dark complexion. All of this lends power and mystery to the work even today. Adding to the effect of the painting, we are aware that Velazquez has been admired for centuries. His work hangs in museums all over the world, most notably the Prado, and one of the world's preeminent art institutions acquired it for millions.

And so we have it. The designation of *masterpiece* is conferred on Velazquez's *Juan de Pareja* both intrinsically as a superb painting and extrinsically as an object of great monetary value. But what of John King's *Frozen Face*?

Placing John King's painting side by side with the Velazquez might be considered audacious or even facetious. It is neither. It is to call attention to the elusiveness of absolutes in art and at the same time underscore the quality of John King's work.

In exploring the nature of creativity, May makes the distinction between creativity that results in genuine art and that which results in *decoration*. Genuine art, he argues, includes at least two indispensable elements— "heightened awareness" and "intensity of encounter." Who would dispute the high sense of awareness expressed in this painting of the *masking* phenomenon (the immobility of the facial muscles) that affects some people with Parkinson's? And who would doubt that the painting is the result of a courageous and highly charged confrontation between John King, who himself has Parkinson's, and this condition?

The gaze of Juan de Pareja holds the viewer transfixed. The same is true of the gaze of *Frozen Face*. Pareja's poise contrasts with the King figure's startled look. The eyes radiate fright and surprise. *What's happened to me? Why am I here?* It is the startled, helpless, and even oddly comical—*Who? Me?*—look we would all feel if we were suddenly faced with a serious affliction, an inexplicable calamity.

It is to its credit that *Frozen Face* does not depict a face of ice or static or distorted facial features. That would have been obvious and therefore less affecting as an *encounter* between the artist and the subject and the subject with the viewer. It would not have conveyed "the shock of the new" as so much of art must. Instead the face is wrapped in what looks like cloth or linen, suggestive of a mummy's shroud. King is making us feel that there is a face *behind* the mask. It is the outer covering that is immobile. Behind it is a *real* face as if to say, "Parkinson's has me bound up, but it does not have *me*." Much of the art produced by people living with Parkinson's who posted on the Parkinson's Disease Foundation website deals with themes related to the illness. Like John King, they confront the illness head-on.

Another approach on the basis of informal observation seems more prevalent. It simply disregards Parkinson's in the work altogether. The creative process becomes a declaration of independence from Parkinson's. Parkinson's is banished, or more accurately, it vanishes. One artist assured me that she paints each day but is not always certain at what time that can happen. Therefore, she needs to be "alert" and "prepared to paint" at any time the medications "kick in."[12] John Fasulo, lifelong photographer who specialized in railroading, a precarious subject for one with limitations in mobility, admitted to needing to be more prudent now in the choices of vantage points for his shots.[13] The richness and lyricism of his photographs, however, remain unaffected.

Thus, for people living with Parkinson's disease, the pursuit of creativity requires—as is the case with all artists—a mastery of a medium but presents its own inventive set of impediments. Some seem almost diabolically ironic. One writer, for example, suddenly found that she could no longer type. Having lost dexterity in her fingers, she lost her job and means of expression all in a single calamity. Undaunted, she turned to painting, a pursuit she had long ago abandoned. She discovered she could hold the brush in her stiffened hand while she could direct her brushstrokes as precisely and delicately as needed by the movement of her shoulder. The creative work of people living with Parkinson's is not merely art created but art *hard-won*. Each work is a victory.

Birch trees and aspens have been a favorite subject of painters and poets. They seem to come easily and often to the aesthetic imagination. Perhaps their stark whiteness set as it often is among the browns and greens of a surrounding wood evokes the notion of nature in its most pristine state. Or maybe the unhurried back-and-forth dance of birches in the wind gives rise to dreamy thoughts. There is, too, in the drawing of a tree or in the writing about it a sense of growth as trunk and limbs in their turn are rendered. Here is John Ruskin, the nineteenth-century English artist, describing an episode in which he drew an aspen near Fontainebleau in 1842. His absorption in his work, particularly the shedding of physical weariness, has much to say about the liberating effect of the creative act among people with Parkinson's.

> Languidly, but not idly, I began to draw it; and as I drew, the languor passed away. The beautiful lines insisted on being traced—without weariness. More and more beautiful they became, as each rose out of the rest, and took its place in the air. With wonder increasing every instant, I saw that they "composed" themselves, by finer

laws than any known to men. At last the tee was there, and everything I had thought before about trees, nowhere.

—John Ruskin[14]

The paintings of birch trees that follows were produced by artists with Parkinson's disease. The verse is Robert Frost's.

Lillian Snyder, *"Birch Tree"*

When I see birches bend to left and right
Across the lines of straighter darker trees,
I like to think some boy's been swinging them.
But swinging doesn't bend them down to stay
As ice storms do. Often you must have seen them
Loaded with ice a sunny winter morning
After a rain...
... One could do worse than be a swinger of birches.

—Robert Frost, from *Birches*[15]

Artists living with Parkinson's are swingers of birches.

Art does not always come to us whole but in fragments. Western art and culture is built on a foundation of potshards, broken tablets, stone and marble rubble, stray pieces of statuary here, and broken busts there. It is sometimes that way, I've found, with the poetry and prose of people with Parkinson's. Parkinson's is a very visual disease. We *see* its manifestations more readily than we read or hear its narrative, which is sometimes difficult to convey as it slowly pilfers our words.

And yet the words come, and even just a few fragments from writers with Parkinson's demonstrate that losses can be slight. The following are samples of work by people with Parkinson's that are juxtaposed with the work of widely known artists. They seem to share common ground yet each has a unique voice.

> One thing at a time,
> Has become a motto of mine.
> I have to break each task down into single moves

—Jackie Barzeley, "I Wish I Knew Why"[16]

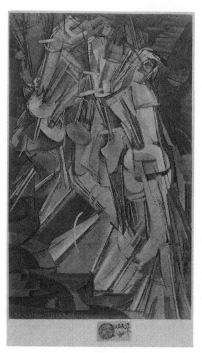

Marcel Duchamp, "Nude Descending a Staircase",
bpk, Berlin/ Art Resource

"Mark Rothko, *"Light Red Over Black"*,
Tate, London/Art Resource, NY

Colors flood the morning sky
Blood red catches my eye
It filters through my fevered mind
Cruel and viciously unkind.

—Robert Canning, from *Blood Red*[7]

I have Parkinson's and the trimmings that
go with it.
It will progress and who knows what
Hopefully science will catch up.
It will be what it is.
There isn't anyone to blame, nor be ashamed but to
deal with it.
Some days yes.

Some days no.
I'm lucky.
I can feel what Monet felt.
I paint.
And that is neat.

—John King, *Neat*[18]

Pierre-Auguste Renoir, *"Young Girls at the Piano"*, HIP/Art Resource, NY

Singing off key, crying off cue,
Feeling off balance
thoughts and words askew
I ask you,
Do you know who she is?
Tone-deaf but loving you,
still, is how it is.[19]

—Trish Bissell

The desire to create arises from deep and seemingly inexhaustible springs. It is a very human effort to reach toward perfection, to find the truth of something even if that something is a flower petal or the menace of distant thunder. It is a search for beauty and an engagement with "the mystery of things."

A thing of beauty is a joy forever:
Its loveliness increases; it will never
Pass into nothingness; but still will keep
A bower quiet for us. And a sleep
Full of sweet dreams, and health, and quiet breathing.
Therefore, in every morrow, are we wreathing
A flowery band to bind us to the earth,

Spite of despondence, of the inhuman dearth
Of noble natures, of gloomy days,
Of all the unhealthy and o'er darkened ways
Made for our searching: yes, in spite of all,
Some shape of beauty moves away the pall
From our dark spirits. Such the sun, the moon,
Trees old, and young, sprouting a shady boon
For simple sleep; and such are daffodils
With the green world they live in; and clear rills
That for themselves a cooling covert make
"Gainst the hot season; the mid forest brake,
Rich with a sprinkling of fair musk rose blooms:
And such too is the grandeur of the dooms
We have imagined for the mighty dead;
All lovely tales that we have heard or read:
An endless fountain of immortal drink,
Pouring into us from the heaven's brink.

—John Keats, from *Endymion*[20]

There cannot be a more passionate proponent of art as indispensable to life itself than John Keats. But of course, he was a poet of the early nineteenth century, untouched by the nihilism of the twentieth century during which art stood pathetic and helpless as God was declared dead and human depravity rendered the world spiritually lifeless. Yet even in that battered state of humanity, the devil himself cannot diminish the value of art as sustenance.

In Nathaniel West's satirical and wrenching novel *Miss Lonelyhearts*, there is a passage about art that West gives over to a character who embodies the basest cynicism imaginable. The novel revolves around an advice-to-the-lovelorn male newspaper writer who, as Miss Lonelyhearts, serves up platitudes but begins to be affected by the broken and barren lives of those who write to him. His editor, Shrike, is as unfeeling and amoral as Lucifer himself. Coming as it does from the thoroughly corrupted soul of Shrike, his debasement of art is turned on its head and becomes a benediction:

But before he [Miss Loneleyhearts] had written a dozen words, Shrike leaned over his shoulder.

"The same old stuff," Shrike said. "Why don't you give them something new and hopeful? Tell them about art. Here, I'll dictate:

'Art Is a Way Out. Do not let life overwhelm you. When the old paths are choked with the debris of failure, look for newer and fresher paths. Art is such a path. Art is distilled from suffering. As Mr. Polnikoff exclaimed through his fine Russian beard, when, at the age of eighty-six, he gave up his business to learn Chinese, "We are, as yet, only at the beginning…"

'Art Is One of the Richest Offerings.

For those who have not the talent to create, there is appreciation. For those…

'Go on from there.'

—Nathaniel West, *Miss Loneleyhearts*[21]

These words from Shrike—from a Lucifer who would deaden the human soul—are true because he would have us believe they are false.

CHAPTER 11

Re-Inventing the Self

Pablo Picasso, *"Woman in Red and Green Striped Beret"*,
Art Resource, NY

"Who are YOU?" said the Caterpillar.

This was not an encouraging opening for a conversation. Alice replied, rather shyly, "I–I hardly know, sir, just at present—at least I know who I WAS when I got up this morning, but I think I must have been changed several times since then."

"What do you mean by that?" said the Caterpillar sternly. "Explain yourself!"

"I can't explain MYSELF, I'm afraid, sir," said Alice, "because I'm not myself, you see."

"I don't see," said the Caterpillar.

"I'm afraid I can't put it more clearly," Alice replied very politely, "for I can't understand it myself to begin with; and being so many different sizes in a day is very confusing."

"It isn't," said the Caterpillar.

"Well, perhaps you haven't found it so yet," said Alice; "but when you have to turn into a chrysalis—you will some day, you know—and then after that into a butterfly, I should think you'll feel it a little queer, won't you?"

"Not a bit," said the Caterpillar.

"Well, perhaps your feelings may be different,' said Alice; 'all I know is, it would feel very queer to ME."

"You!" said the Caterpillar contemptuously. "Who are YOU?"

Which brought them back again to the beginning of the conversation.

—Lewis Carroll, *Alice's Adventures in Wonderland*[1]

Of the many larcenies Parkinson's disease is capable of committing, the grandest of all is theft of the self. A diagnosis of Parkinson's often leads to the loss of a job, the dissolution of relationships, and the gradual erosion of the vigor and animating qualities we associate with identity and personality. Those who were providers find it increasingly difficult to provide. Mothers who were primary caregivers gradually become dependents themselves. And fathers whose steady hands on the tiller gave such comfort to their families now may need more comforting than their pride can bear. Slowly but inexorably, a mask—literally and figuratively—descends upon the person with Parkinson's. It is all one can do to hold on to what once was whole and recognizable before the pieces begin to harden, crack, and are lost.

Parkinson's disease—as are all serious chronic and degenerative illnesses—is not an additive condition. It is transformative. It is not life *plus* Parkinson's but a new life altogether. Familiar markers might remain. The lawn still needs mowing. The stairs still lead up to the bedroom. The car is still in the garage. The children still ask for help with homework. But our relationship to each of these things has changed. We are not the same.

And if we are not the same, then who are we?

The shattering of identity that the sudden discovery of a serious illness can sometimes cause is captured vividly by Alexander Solzhenitsyn in a passage from his autobiographical, *The Cancer Ward.*

> The hard lump of his tumour—unexpected, meaningless, and quite without use—had dragged him like a fish on a hook and flung him into this iron bed—a narrow, mean bed with creaking springs and an apology for a mattress. Having once undressed said goodbye to the family and came up to the ward, you felt that the door to all your past life had been slammed behind you.
>
> —Alexander Solzhenitsyn, *The Cancer Ward*[2]

As powerful as this image is, there is not in all of literature a transformation more analogous to the experience of a devastating diagnosis than that of the protagonist of one of the great novels of the twentieth century. The novel begins,

> As Gregor Samsa awoke one morning from a troubled dream he found himself transformed in his bed into a monstrous insect. He was lying on his hard, as it were armor-plated, back and when he lifted his head a little he could see his dome-like brown belly divided into corrugated segments on top of which the bed quilt could hardly keep in position and was about to slide off completely. His numerous legs, which were pitifully thin compared to the rest of his bulk flimmered helplessly before his eyes. "What has happened to me?" he thought. "It was no dream."
>
> —Franz Kafka, *The Metamorphosis*[3]

The story takes place at the turn of the twentieth century somewhere in Germany. Gregor Samsa is a dutiful young man who supports his father, mother, and sister, each of whom is a failure and displays varying degrees of ingratitude toward Gregor. They all live together in the same apartment, and upon discovering Gregor's transformation into a giant insect, his parents and sister are repelled by him. Things become worse when he begins to lose mobility, and soon his speech becomes indistinct as well. As a result of an injury caused by his father, Gregor begins to weaken and die, and his family facilitates his death, to which they are indifferent. Despite knowing that Gregor indeed metamorphosed into an insect, they rationalize that the creature was not Gregor at all but was in fact a giant insect.

As Vladimir Nabokov has observed, Gregor was a human being disguised as an insect who lived among insects disguised as people.[4] The carapace in which Gregor was trapped distorted his body but did not diminish his "utter unselfishness, his constant preoccupation with others ... and [his] ... subtle human nature."[5] Kafka has turned the world upside down. The *normal* and *conventional* parents are revealed to be grotesque while the ostensibly bizarre and grossly abnormal Gregor Samsa upholds human values and virtue. Gregor lost his body but did not lose his self or his soul.

The irony in Kafka's story is that despite Gregor's physical metamorphosis, his humanity remains intact. There is a continuity of his character before and after the external change. His essential goodness endures. By contrast, the craven selfishness of the parents and especially his sister, Grete, becomes magnified as Gregor's predicament grows more dire. Gregor's physical metamorphosis precipitates *their* moral decay, not his. Kafka seems to be saying that dramatic outward change—of appearance, of circumstance, of fortune—extends and enlarges what is already the character within us.

For Kafka, the fecklessness and self-absorption of other people—even those we rely upon to validate our identity—renders them unreliable. It is heart-rending when even Grete, the sister whom Gregor trusted implicitly, strips him of the remaining shreds of his selfhood as Gregor the person and Gregor the brother. "You must try to get rid of the idea that this is Gregor," she tells her parents. "The fact that we've believed it for so long is the root of all our trouble. But how can it be Gregor? If this were Gregor, he would have realized long ago that human beings can't live with such a creature, and he'd have gone away on his own accord."[6]

Here Kafka illuminates what may be the greatest fear of people with a transforming illness. It is not merely the fear of losing one's sense of self. As painful as this may be, the real nightmare is what we cannot control—the way in which others see us. We might insist that despite our illness, we are who we always have been, but this can be met with incredulity. Some invisible line may be crossed at which point we cannot reconcile both what we *have become* and what we *were*. It is not because it would be impossible for us to exist in this duality but because it would be impossible for others to accept.

As was the case with Gregor Samsa and his family, the construction of our senses of selves took place long before any physical metamorphosis induced by Parkinson's disease. It is not possible now to create a new edifice. We must build from what is already there.

William Barrett, a contemporary philosopher and scholar draws a clear distinction between the public aspect of our everyday existence on the one hand and on the other, a more private, deeper, and meaningful *self* that we have created for ourselves. He refers to the public person as "the One," meaning that we are one of many Americans, students, mothers, fathers, or Parkinson's patients.

> The One is the impersonal and public creature whom each of us is even before he is an I. One has such-and-such a manner, one does this, one does not do that, etc., etc. … So long as we remain in the womb of this externalized and public existence, we are spared the terror and the dignity of becoming the self.

> —William Barrett, *Irrational Man*[7]

It is "the One" that breaks most readily with a diagnosis of Parkinson's. We can no longer do such-and-such the way we have always done it. We are no longer one among many colleagues on the job. We can no longer do this or that in the same manner. We become, with or without our assent, one very different from the one we used to be. We have awakened, like Gregor Samsa, from a troubled dream to find ourselves physically transformed. But it is no dream.

Barrett points out that real life—mortality, anxiety, illness—intrudes upon the "sheltered position" of the one and forces us to confront the self. The self is the part of us that is the most enduring, the wellspring of our strength and a connection to our authentic existence. For most people going about their daily business, it is much easier to be a *one* if only because, as Barrett observes, "the modern world has wonderfully multiplied all the devices of self-evasion."[8]

For people living with Parkinson's, however, self-evasion is no longer possible. Life has intruded. We must at last confront our sense of self. The "wonderfully multiplied devices for self-evasion" have now lost much of their power of seduction in the face of a new reality. Joseph Campbell seems to sense precisely our challenge.

Some people are late bloomers, and come to particular stages at a relatively late age. You have to have a feeling for where you are. You've got only one life to live, and you don't have to live it for six people. Pay attention to it.

—Joseph Campbell[9]

In Shakespeare's monumental *King Lear*, Lear has come to one of those "particular stages" of life at a very late age indeed. Until then, he had "but slenderly known [himself]."[10] The breaking apart and reassembling of Lear as a king, a man, and a father is a journey of self-discovery that is astonishing in its depth of understanding of the human soul. Many regard *King Lear* as Shakespeare's greatest artistic achievement. For those of us who—late or soon—seek to lead an examined life, it is a revelation.

King Lear is set in Britain centuries before the introduction of Christianity. At the very start of the play, Lear is a man whose most prominent quality is the certainty of his own importance and the preeminence of his will. However, acknowledging his advanced age and desirous of being free of the responsibilities of state, he has decided to divide his kingdom equally among his three daughters, Goneril, Regan, and his youngest and favorite, Cordelia. Before he bestows the gift of dominion to each of them, however, and in an act of typical vanity, he asks that each daughter describe how much she loves him. Goneril and Regan flatter him effusively. Cordelia alone answers Lear honestly, "I love your Majesty/According to my bond, no more no less."[11]

At this, Lear flies into a rage. He effectively banishes Cordelia and the earl of Kent, who attempts to talk sense to him. As the plot unfolds, Lear is betrayed by the daughters he so blindly and foolishly rewarded for their self-serving flattery, gradually stripped by them of his royal prerogatives and literally thrown out into a monstrous storm where he finds himself destitute and reduced to living in a barely human state. Lear descends into utter despair and madness but survives the storm thanks to the help of Kent (in disguise) and the king's loyal fool. In the end, Goneril and Regan's byzantine plots to usurp each other's power destroy them, and Cordelia is reunited with Lear. Their reconciliation is short-lived. Cordelia is murdered by a paid assassin of Edmund, who (in a subplot of the play) has schemed against his brother Edgar for his inheritance. The evil Edmund allied himself with Goneril and Regan against Lear and his own father, the earl of Gloucester. While rightful political succession is achieved in the end, both Lear and Cordelia die. We are left to ponder and in some sense recover from a dramatic tour de force of human vanity, venality, love, madness, and despair.

There are certain errors of judgment we make that cannot be undone or redeemed. Lear's unbounded vanity and need to be revered impels him to accept Goneril and Regan's false avowals of love and to reject Cordelia's genuine fealty despite his deep love for her. This decision costs him his kingdom, his selfhood, Cordelia, and his life.

Lear's torments begin not by chance or fate but by an act of his own will, and in this, our experience (an unbidden illness) and Lear's are very different. Yet we are no less in danger of losing our sense of self to illness than Lear is in losing his to his own folly and the cruelty of his two daughters. They quickly strip him of the trappings of royal privilege and position. Until recently, his selfhood had been defined by a crown, but it's now reduced to being derided as senile and treated with contempt. His humiliation increases. In a fit of rage, he curses Goneril, wishing her sterility, or if she should give birth, then he would have it be a child who causes tears to "fret channels in her cheeks." In a pathetic expression of self-pity, Lear declares, "How sharper than a serpent's tooth it is/To have a thankless child."[12]

Lear has made the mistake of allowing his vanity or perhaps his fear of *not* being loved in his dotage to cloud his judgment in discerning friend from foe. He disowns Cordelia, banishes his trusted servant the earl of Kent, and embraces his doom in the persons of Goneril and Regan. Lear quickly finds that he is no longer the person he supposed himself to be. He is no longer a king but a doddering old man who needs to be fed and led, and he's in no position to make demands on anyone. As Regan supports her sister Goneril's refusal to provide Lear with his usual retinue of knights, she speaks to Lear and verbally plunges a dagger into the heart of one whose self has until now been defined as king, patriarch, and man of power. That man no longer exists.

> [Regan]: O, sir, you are old,
>   Nature in you stands on the very verge
> Of his confine. You should be rul'd and led
> By some discretion that discerns your state
>   Better than you yourself.[13]

Lear is not so much demeaned by his daughters as discarded by them as a nonperson. As a fierce storm approaches, he is left to fend for himself against the elements. Here on a storm-torn British heath, Shakespeare expresses with unparalleled dramatic force the discovery of self through the illuminating power of despair.

As the storm rages, Lear's fury is still directed at his daughters. Ever the imperious king, he absolves nature of any responsibility for his current state or of any obligation to set things right. The forces that have brought him down are not nature's but his daughters' malevolence. Yet his sights are still confined to his own misfortune.

> [Lear]: Rumble thy bellyful! Spit, fire! Spout, rain!
>   Nor rain, wind, thunder, fire are my daughters
>   I tax not you, elements, with unkindness;
>   I never gave you kingdom, called you children;
>   You owe me no subscription. Then let fall
>   Your horrible pleasure. Here I stand your slave
>   A poor, infirm, weak and despis'd old man.[14]

****

> I am a man
> More sinn'd against than sinning.[15]

However, the further Lear descends into despair and the fiercer grows the storm, the closer he comes to the truth. He begins to see that railing against the causes of his disastrous state is useless, and worse, it will cost him his sanity. To the loyal Kent (who remains disguised, caring for Lear on the heath), he says,

> [Lear:] "No, I will weep no more. In such a night
> To shut me out? Pour on, I will endure.
> In such a night as this? O Regan, Goneril!
> Your old kind father, whose frank heart gave all—
> O, that way madness lies, let me shun that!
> No more of that."[16]

To fixate on the past, to allow oneself to be trapped in a prison of recrimination and self-pity is to literally lose one's *self* "that way madness lies." The challenge he has—the challenge we all have—is to endure "in such a night as this."

Following close upon this exchange, Lear begins to show a glimmer of empathy he had failed to sufficiently exhibit as king, absorbed as he was in the trappings of his exalted office. The "pitiless storm" evokes his sympathy for "poor naked wretches, wheresoe'er you are" as he realizes that "[he's] taken too little care of this!"[17]

In Lear's spiritual and physical journey on the roiling heath, clothing—the condition of it, the wearing of it, our nakedness without it—becomes a metaphor for the conventions of civilization and its capacity for suppressing the self. As William Barrett observed, society provides us with a multiplicity of wonderful means for self-evasion. Clothing (i.e., outward appearances) Lear refers to now as "lendings" and begins to strip himself bare despite the howling storm. He sees now that his royal station was a carapace (not unlike that of Gregor Samsa), while the self is hidden and distorted by the contrivances we create for our social structures. His epiphany comes as he tears off his clothes. "Thou art the thing itself: unaccommodated man is no more but such a poor, bare, fork'd animal … Off, off you lendings!"[18]

As Lear makes his journey from a coddled king possessing everything to a storm-tossed man possessing nothing, he comes to know the meaning of true familial love, loyalty, and an identity built on the "truth of the thing itself" rather than falsehoods. He has come to embody Sartre's assertion—preempted by Shakespeare by about four hundred years—that "human life begins on the far side of despair."[19] Lear's reconciliation with Cordelia (who has returned from France with an army to restore Lear to the throne) is excruciating in its poignancy. Severely weakened by his ordeal, Lear turns to Cordelia and says, "You must bear with me./Pray you now forget, and forgive; I am old and foolish."[20] Such an admission would have been unthinkable at the opening of the play.

As Goneril and Regan's forces temporarily gain the upper hand, Lear and Cordelia are captured and remanded to prison. Lear is unfazed. He has found himself, and he has been reunited with his beloved daughter. He imagines that they need nothing but each other as they spend their days in a new world of their own creation.

> Come let's away to prison:
> We two alone will sing like birds I' th' cage;
> When thou dost ask me blessing, I'll kneel down
> And ask thee forgiveness. So we'll live,
> And pray, and sing, and tell old tales, and laugh
> At gilded butterflies, and hear poor rogues
> Talk of court news; and we'll talk with them too—
> Who loses and who wins; who's in, who's out,
>   And take upon 's the mystery of things
> As if we were God's spies; and we'll wear out,
> In a wall'd prison packs and sets of great ones,
> That ebb and flow by the moon.[21]

The irony of this fantasy is that this life could have been possible when Lear was *King* Lear. But he was a very different person then. He has come to himself too late to save himself or Cordelia. But in the final tally, this does not diminish the importance of his own metamorphosis. He managed to throw off "the One" and take on "the Self," and in doing so, he became a more genuine person. This achievement is its own reward. *King Lear* does not end happily, but it ends fittingly.

What, after all, has been gained by Lear? What, after all, do we have to gain by his example?

The answer has more to do with the manner in which we choose to conduct our lives than it does with the outcome, which in every case is the same. Michel de Montaigne might just as well have been reflecting upon Lear when he wrote in his essay "Experience." "Have you learned to compose your character? Have you learned to lay hold of repose? [Then] you have done more than he who has laid hold of empires and cities. Man's great and glorious master-work is to live befittingly; all other things—to reign, to lay up treasure, to build—are at the best mere accessories and aids."[22]

To live befittingly demands much from us. It is, Montaigne warns, "a rugged road, more so than it seems, to follow a pace so rambling and uncertain, as that of the soul; to penetrate the dark profundities of its internal windings; to choose and lay hold of so many little nimble motions; 'tis a new and extraordinary undertaking."[23]

Montaigne helped teach the West the art of the closely examined life— the kind of life that Socrates, nearly two millennia earlier, declared to be the only life worth living. Writing of Montaigne's lifelong quest, Virginia Woolf makes clear the nature of the rewards,

> For beyond the difficulty of communicating oneself, there is the supreme difficulty of being oneself. This soul, or life within us, by no means agrees with the life outside us … The man who is aware of himself is henceforward independent; and he is never bored, and life is only too short, and he is steeped through and through with a profound yet tempered happiness. He alone lives, while other people, slaves of ceremony, let life slip past them in a kind of dream.[24]

CHAPTER 12

The Moment

Frederic Church, *"Sunset"* Munson-Williams-
Proctor Art Institute/Art Resource, NY

Most of the big shore places were closed now and there
were hardly any lights except the shadowy, moving glow of
a ferryboat across the Sound. And as the moon rose high
the inessential houses began to melt away until gradually
I became aware of the old island here that flowered once
for the Dutch sailors' eyes—a fresh green breast of the
new world. Its vanished trees, the trees that gave way for
Gatsby's house, had once pandered in whispers to the
last and greatest of all human dreams: for a transitory
enchanted moment man must have held his breath in the

presence of this continent, compelled into an aesthetic contemplation he neither understood nor desired, face to face for the last time in history with something commensurate to his capacity for wonder.

—F. Scott Fitzgerald, *The Great Gatsby*[1]

It is a commonplace—but no less significant for being one –to take the view that our lives are lived entirely in the present. The past no longer exists, and the future itself is known only when it becomes the present. The continuous *flow* of our lives is an illusion. Life comes to us piecemeal as a succession of moments, sometimes quickening, sometimes slowing. But always it is the now. Hemingway is at his most unsentimental when he puts it this way:

> That is all your whole life is, now. There is nothing else than now. There is neither yesterday, certainly, nor is there any tomorrow. How old must you be before you know that? There is only now, and if now is only two days, then two days is your life and everything in it will be in proportion. This is how to live a life in two days. And if you stop complaining and asking for what you will never get, you will have a good life. A good life is not measured in any span.[2]

With all due respect to Hemingway and many others who hold a similar view, I would argue that it is not true that "there is neither yesterday ... nor ... any tomorrow." Memories bring the past into the present and thereby make the present different than it might otherwise be without those memories. Likewise, what we imagine for the future necessarily colors our experience of the now. Therefore, the *now* that Hemingway speaks of is not a thing unto itself but a reality seen through the prism of time. Separating facets from one another so that there is nothing else but the present asks the mind to do the nearly impossible—to function in an unconnected middle ground, an island untouched by a sea of time.

Yet that unconnected place is where many of us find ourselves. On one side of it, memories vanish and can't be coaxed into the present. No matter how hard we pull on the door, it stays jammed shut. On the other far side, the future appears forbidding. We'd rather not look. By force of circumstance as well as by our own design, we *are* in the moment, in what Vladimir Nabokov called that "brief crack of light between two eternities."[3] Of what use can we make of that brief crack of light?

Great artists have recognized the power of a closely felt moment to move us and give our lives meaning if we are willing to stay within it and really *see* it. James Joyce's *A Portrait of the Artist as a Young Man* (with young protagonist Stephan Dedalus) is a thinly veiled chronicle of Joyce's early development as a writer. The story is told as a succession of remembered events, one of which is an encounter with a beautiful woman of his acquaintance on a tram after leaving a party. This passage exemplifies the ability of an artist like Joyce to savor a single moment and express it with such perfect pitch and precision that it is fully lived by the writer and the reader. It is a relatively long passage, and it is reproduced here in its entirety so that the coherence of the moment is not broken.

It was the last tram. The lank brown horses knew it and shook their bells to the clear night in admonition. The conductor talked with the driver, both nodding often in the green light of the lamp. On the empty seats of the tram were scattered a few coloured tickets. No sound of footsteps came up or down the road. No sound broke the peace of the night save when the lank brown horses rubbed their noses together and shook their bells.

> They seemed to listen, he on the upper step and she on the lower. She came up to his step many times and went down to hers again between their phrases and once or twice stood close beside him for some moments on the upper step, forgetting to go down, and then going down. His heart danced upon her movements like a cork upon a tide. He heard what her eyes said to him from beneath their cowl and knew that in some dim past, whether in life or in reverie, he had heard their tale before. He saw her

urge her vanities, her fine dress and sash and long black stockings, and knew that he yielded to them a thousand times. Yet a voice within him spoke above the noise of his dancing heart, asking him would he take her gift to which he had only to stretch out his hand. And he remembered the day when he and Eileen had stood looking into the hotel grounds, watching the waiters running up a trail of bunting on the flagstaff and the fox terrier scampering to and fro on the sunny lawn and how, all of a sudden, she had broken out into a peal of laughter and had run down the sloping curve of the path. Now, as then, he stood listlessly in his place, seemingly a tranquil watcher of the scene before him.

She too wants me to catch hold of her, he thought. That's why she came with me to the tram. I could easily catch hold of her when she comes up to my step: nobody is looking. I could hold her and kiss her.

But he did neither: and, when he was sitting alone on the deserted tram he tore his ticket into shreds and stared gloomily at the corrugated floorboard.

—James Joyce, *A Portrait of the Artist as a Young Man*[4]

Joyce's moment on the tram, like all moments worth living and remembering, is a landscape of emotion and narrative texture. Things happen. We see things close up. We imagine the hand reaching out and holding still. The up-and-down of the tram steps, the shredding of the ticket, and the corrugated floorboard all create a moment that is alive. It is great art as well as a primer on what it means to "be in the moment" as a person simply living one's life with eyes wide open.

Virginia Woolf makes this same point writing of Joseph Conrad's narrator, Marlow, who recognizes the power of the sudden insight, the flash of light shining on an incident. Woolf tells of Marlow overhearing a French military officer exclaim "how the time passes" and then cites Marlow's reaction.

> Nothing [he comments] could have been more commonplace than this remark; but its utterance coincided for me [Marlow] with a moment of vision. It's extraordinary how we go through life with eyes half shut, with dull ears, with dormant thoughts ... Nevertheless, there can be but few of us who had never known one of these rare moments of awakening, when we see, hear, understand, ever so much—everything—in a flash.
>
> —Virginia Woolf, "Joseph Conrad" in *The Common Reader*[5]

Perhaps the grandmaster of the fully realized moment in literature second only to Shakespeare is Marcel Proust. Proust's eight-volume novel *Remembrance of Things Past* is an undisputed masterpiece of twentieth-century fiction. Unjustifiably, it has become a symbol of the ponderous, character-laden, plotless work that is force-fed to college literature majors in defiance of our speed-addicted world. Those who do venture to read Proust, however, will find a rich and often riveting chronicle of human character, love, time, memory, social intrigue, and loss.

Proust constructs his narrative from a succession of memories of his own life often prompted by a sensual stimulus that opens the floodgates of remembrances. The familiar taste of a sweet cake triggers recollections of his childhood in Combray. A strain of music recalls an affair. The ringing of a bell evokes a sad event decades earlier. Proust's work is, above all, about people and reaffirms Emerson's remark to the effect that "there is properly no history, only biography."[6] The structure of Proust's work is determined by his recollection of people, their sensibilities, and their relationships. "Proustian detail" has come to mean the closest possible observation and the greatest possible appreciation of the essence of people and the events that constitute our lives. Writing of her year of reading Proust, Phyllis Rose describes "Proustian detail" as "slowly, patiently, imaginatively, thoroughly, bringing everything in his mind to bear one each observation, comparing, contrasting, contextualizing, historicizing, drawing out of his inner darkness the precise words needed to render the emotion in all its particularity as it's never been rendered in words before."[7]

It is easy enough to say that somewhere between a work of genius such as *Remembrance of Things Past* and total inattentiveness to "the moment" is a halfway mark at which ordinary people—especially those with Parkinson's—should take careful note of things with something approximating Proustian detail. And yet it seems that as we get older, we're more apt to allow these moments to pass unexamined and underappreciated, to take them for granted.

The novelist Saul Bellow offers an explanation. As we age, "we become too familiar with the data of experience" and eliminate "the details that bewitch, hold, or delay children."[8] Bellow, I think, is referring to a "been there, done that" mind-set that affects our engagement level with experiences and almost by default leads the older mind to fast-forward to the next moment. Thus, time for us seems to move quickly while for children it slows down. They remain in the moment because the moment for them is so new. We've seen the movie before and are quick to move on. But what's the rush? C. V. Cavafy, a Greek poet of the first half of the twentieth century, likened our own passage through life to that of Odysseus's journey home to Ithaca. Odysseus's journey was delayed involuntarily. Cavafy urges us to delay ours deliberately.

> As you set out for Ithacahope your road is a long one, full of adventure, full of discovery.
> … May there be many summer mornings when, with what pleasure, what joy, you enter harbors you're seeing for the first time; may you stop at Phoenician trading stations to buy fine things, mother of pearl and coral, amber and ebony. sensual perfume of every kind—
> as many sensual perfumes as you can;
> … Keep Ithaca always in your mind. Arriving there is what you're destined for.

But don't hurry the journey at all.
Better if it lasts for years,
... Ithaca gave you the marvelous journey... And if you
find her poor, Ithaca won't have fooled you.
Wise as you will have become, so full of experience,
you'll have understood by then what these Ithakas mean.

—C. V. Cavafy, from "Ithaca"[9]

CHAPTER 13

Fear

Berlin Painter (6th-5th BCE), *"Medusa"*, The Trustees
of the British Museum, Art Resource/NY

Nothing easier than to say, Have no fear! Nothing more
difficult. How does one kill fear, I wonder? How do you
shoot a spectre through the heart, slash off its spectral
head, take it by its spectral throat? It is an enterprise you
rush into when you dream, and are glad to make your
escape with wet hair and every limb shaking. The bullet
is not run, the blade not forged, the man not born; even
the winged words of truth drop at your feet like lumps

of lead. You require for such a desperate encounter an enchanted and poison shaft dipped in a lie too subtle to be found on earth.

—Joseph Conrad, *Lord Jim*[1]

There is little point in urging ourselves to have no fear. The kind of fear we experience in reaction to a sudden occurrence, for example, is reflexive and not entirely within our control. It seems to be part of a primal system of vigilance—an early signal of danger that can prompt us either to flee or to stand and fight. This kind of fear erupts unbidden when we suddenly lose sight of our child in a park or when a plane in which we're traveling drops a thousand feet in a storm. Courage can be reflexive, too, but we rarely feel it as an eruption. Courage feels as if it is more a matter of volition. We can summon it, and we can build it up. It is fortifying and under control. Reflexive fear, on the other hand, once it takes hold, can quickly overwhelm us.

Another kind of fear—the kind that seeps through our defenses and chills us to the bone and never dissipates—is the sort of fear that settles in as an abiding presence rather than being a reaction to a specific occurrence. In our waking hours, we might feel it as a cold wind that kicks up from time to time, and in our dreams it transforms itself like an incubus into shadowy figures or harrowing falls from cliffs or betrayals or any number of disturbances of psychic peace. It is the sort of fear that can come with living with Parkinson's disease.

Raymond Carver, recognized primarily as one of America's masters of the short story, also wrote poetry. Here he gives voice to many of his own fears, but he seems to feel one more acutely than the others.

> ….Fear of seeing a police car pull into the drive. Fear of falling asleep at night.
> Fear of not falling asleep.
> Fear of the past rising up.
> Fear of the present taking flight.
> Fear of the telephone that rings in the dead of night.

Fear of electrical storms.

Fear of the cleaning woman who has a spot on her cheek!...

—from Raymond Carver, "Fear"[2]

Carver confesses to having the primordial fear everyone experiences—the fear of death. He does so obliquely, almost slyly, as if to avoid the pain of facing it head-on. That fear comes at the bottom of his list, not the top as we might expect. In a deliberately transparent attempt to disguise its real prominence in the pantheon of his fears, he repeats "fear of death" absentmindedly as if it were trivial. It is not, of course—not for Carver, not for us, and not for anyone. The fear of death and the pervasive sense of mortality it fuels in us underlie all other fears. It is our knowing that our time is limited that causes us to "Fear this day will end on an unhappy note" (for how many days to we have to squander?) or "Fear of not loving or not loving enough" (for what is the meaning of life if not to love and be loved?). It is the overarching fear of death and the constellation of fears and subterfuges surrounding it that form the basis of some of the richest experiences in literature and art.

Fear is a part of the human condition, an essential part of the organism's natural wiring for survival. There's no escape from it or from the many disturbances it breeds in our lives. There is no remedy given here. How we manage the inevitable is what matters. Edgar, son of the earl of Gloucester and heir to Lear's throne, remarks to his blinded father, "What, in ill thoughts again? Men must endure/Their going hence even as their coming hither. Ripeness is all."[3]

Perhaps it is a small measure of comfort to know that the bravest among us experience fear. Audie Murphy, a Medal of Honor recipient and the most decorated American soldier of World War II, wrote, "I never moved into combat without having the feeling of a cold hand reaching into my guts and twisting them into knots ... I was scared before every battle. That old instinct of self-preservation is a pretty basic thing."[4]

Audie Murphy's admission is as old as war itself. In *The Iliad*, Homer presents us with a portrait of war and heroism unequalled in literature before or since. Hector, the prince of Troy, is a magnificent warrior, an inspiration to his people, beloved of the gods, and up until his fated battle with Achilles, the scourge of the Greeks. Never has he cowered before an enemy. But Achilles is another matter when they finally meet face-to-face outside the walls of Troy.

> ...Achilles was closing on him now
> Like the god of war, the fighter's helmet flashing,
> Over his right shoulder shaking the Pelian ash spear,
> That terror, and the bronze around his body flared
> Like a raging fire or the rising, blazing sun.
> Hector looked up, saw him, started to tremble,
> Nerve gone, he could hold his ground no longer, he left
> the gates behind and away he fled in fear—
> ... so Achilles flew at him, breakneck on in fury—
> With Hector fleeing along the walls of Troy,
> Fast as his legs would go.

—Homer, *The Iliad*[5]

Hector eventually gathers himself and fights and dies with honor. We share in his nobility as well as in his brief and very human lapse into abject fear. Homer is telling us that fear occurs among the most noble mortals and even among the gods themselves. Whatever our fears, they have been the same fears of countless others.

Personal and collective fear has animated human history since our species first appeared in the African gorges or, as many prefer, since Eve bit into the apple. When Adam did the same, God called to him, and Adam replied, "I heard thy voice in the garden, and *I was afraid*, because I was naked; and *I hid myself*" (emphasis mine). [6] Fear was now born in man. Before this point in the Western religious canon, fear did not exist. After the fall, fear was loosed upon the world.

Some fear, of course, is all to the good. "Fear of God" is a term synonymous with faith. And what is faith (whether it is directed toward deities that are real or unreal) but a means of assuaging fear? Most fear is corrosive and enervating and a burden, and we perennially seek to lighten such fear by appealing to a greater power than our own.

Faith in God can certainly dispel fear. So too, we feel the empathy of others, which can ease our fears if not heal our wounds. The connectedness of human beings, despite the sometimes atrocious behavior we display toward one another, is an important virtue in most civilized societies. Joseph Campbell spoke of having been awestruck by the willingness of soldiers in Vietnam to risk their own lives to retrieve a wounded comrade or protect his fellow soldiers. "How can a human being," Campbell asks, "so participate in the peril or pain of another that without a thought, spontaneously, he sacrifices his own life? Schopenhauer says this is the breakthrough of the metaphysical realization that you and the other are one, that you are aspects of the one life."[7]

If Campbell is right, it might explain why for so many people living with Parkinson's and certainly for other people undergoing personal stress draw comfort from support groups. In addition to or even in the absence of close-knit extended families or social units like small towns and villages, the support group provides the connectedness that allows for the sharing or psychological dissipation of stress.

This effect is not much removed from the power of literature and art to alleviate fear. Although literature and art are obviously involved in a much more private interchange, their power also derives from empathy by way of the artist's ability to acknowledge "the peril and pain" of his or her audience. Our deepest fears and darkest places are acknowledged and exposed; our hobgoblins are confronted. On behalf of each of us, the archetypal hero sets out to slay our dragons. Sometimes he succeeds, and sometimes he does not. But the act itself affirms the possibility of salvation. When St. George, as legend holds, slew the dragon that was menacing the water wells of Lydda, he opens up the possibility that *all* dragons can be slain. When Beowulf defeats Grendel, *all* man-eating monsters can be overcome, and if the human mind can conceive of a King Arthur and a Round Table and a Lancelot, then *all of us* can conceive of a moment in which no fear is possible.

...the monster's whole
      body was in pain, a tremendous wound
appeared on his shoulder. Sinews split
and the bone-lappings burst. Beowulf was granted
the glory of winning; Grendel was driven
under the fen-banks, fatally hurt,
to his desolate lair. His days were numbered,
the end of his life was coming over him,
he knew it for certain; and one bloody clash
had fulfilled the dearest wishes of the Danes.
The man who had lately landed among them,
Proud and sure, had purged the hall,
Kept it from harm;...

—from *Beowulf,* translated by Seamus Heaney[8]

CHAPTER 14

Happiness

"Bull Jumping", Minoan Fresco, 1500 BCE. Erich Lessing, Art Resource, NY

And may the good gods give you all your heart desires
Husband and house, and lasting harmony, too.
No finer, greater gift in the world than that...
When man and woman possess their home, two minds,
two hearts that work as one. Despair to their enemies,
joy to all their friends. Their own best claim to glory.

—Homer, *The Odyssey*[1]

Achieving happiness is difficult enough under ordinary circumstances. Being happy while living with Parkinson's sets the bar a lot higher. But Parkinson's disease in and of itself need not make happiness less attainable. Nor is it true, given available evidence, that those things that make people living with Parkinson's happy are different than the things that make everyone else happy. To imagine that we would surely be happy if only we were rid of Parkinson's is an illusion, understandable though it may be. Happiness, closely considered, is more complicated than that ... and simpler.

For a long time, *happiness* in the West did not mean what it means today. Ancient philosophers, most notably Plato, sought a theory of happiness that would apply to every person and lead to a happy life if its precepts were met. Plato's idea, developed throughout his *Dialogues* but especially in *The Republic*, is that happiness is not an end unto itself but the result of a just and virtuous life. A just and good person would necessarily be happy because his or her soul would be free of corruption and in a state of balanced harmony. Pleasure, for the most part, was distinguished from happiness; its single-minded pursuit for its own sake would surely lead to unhappiness because of its disregard of virtue.[2] Aristotle echoed Plato, declaring happiness "the highest good" and arguing that "living well and doing well are the same as being happy," where "doing well" meant living virtuously.[3]

With the rise of Christianity, an important perceptual shift occurred. Christianity's elevation of suffering as redemptive and the promise of paradise in the afterlife in effect declared that happiness here on earth was not only unattainable but suspect. Insofar as one could enjoy happiness at all, it would have to involve genuine spiritual communion with Christ and obedience to the laws of the church.

Somewhere along the historical continuum—perhaps coinciding with the rise of ideas of individualism, self-reliance, and political liberty in the eighteenth and nineteenth centuries—things changed again. Each person could now define happiness for him or herself. The sheriff (moral philosophers, kings and queens, and an omnipotent and ubiquitous church) left town, so to speak. Most importantly, as the industrial revolution and modern technology dramatically raised the standard of living and a vast middle class grew in the West, happiness (1) seemed more the result of accumulating material goods than exemplifying virtue or godliness and (2) became attainable even by the average person. Happiness was democratized. Its achievement was now not only a realistic possibility, but the "pursuit of happiness" became the purpose of life and enshrined by law.

Saul Bellow's novel *Herzog* is certainly not about happiness *per se*, but its opening passage is remarkable in underscoring how far we've come from Plato in terms of our notions of what constitutes happiness.

> If I am out of my mind, it's all right with me, thought Moses Herzog. Some people thought he was cracked and for a time he himself had doubted that he was all there. But now, though he still behaved oddly, he felt confident, cheerful, clairvoyant, and strong. He had fallen under a spell and written letters to everyone under the sun. He was so stirred by these letters that from the end of June he moved from place to place with a valise full of papers ... he wrote endlessly, fanatically, to the newspapers, to people in public life, to friends and relatives and at last to the dead, his own obscure dead, and finally the famous dead.
>
> —Saul Bellow, *Herzog*[4]

It is true, as Bellow himself writes, that some people would consider Herzog "cracked," one of them assuredly being Plato. But two thousand years after *The Dialogues*, who is to say that Moses Herzog isn't happy?

Herzog is not cracked. Nor can it be said that he is happy. But his behavior and comfort with it makes the point that happiness is not a state of being with common denominators for all. It is a very personal, self-defined, and often temporary frame of mind accessible to most people any time in their lives, extending even to those whom some might consider beyond the reach of happiness. This is a fundamental principle in the Western view of happiness. As John Locke argued, human beings must be afforded the freedom to pursue their personal brand of happiness and will act in a way that they believe will ensure it. Of course, some people's choices may prove wrong or misguided, and they must be held accountable then.[5]

Liberated from Plato's version of happiness as a life of virtue and justice and detached also from the strictures of an omnipotent church, happiness could now be defined by the individual. This is what Immanuel Kant called "private happiness." However, even he added a caveat. "Private happiness" has to be governed by moral and ethical laws so that a person becomes *worthy* of it.[6]

Yet our postmodern world dismisses the idea that one must be *worthy* of happiness. Everyone is entitled to it as long as no one gets hurt. Thus, after centuries of theorizing about happiness, we now have more of the things that would seem to make us happy with the added advantage that each of us is permitted to define happiness for ourselves. Shouldn't we then be happier than ever? In fact, we are not. In the industrialized West and America specifically, we are increasingly unhappy and feeling more depressed.[7]

This is not speculation but an empirically supported finding. Serious social and psychological research has been conducted to measure "subjective well-being" (the social sciences' word for happiness). The results are clear and disturbing. We are becoming more dissatisfied with our lives. And this is a finding that applies to the whole population—healthy and ill, young and old, rich and poor, living with Parkinson's or without.

One major study from the Institute of Social Policy Studies headed by Professor Robert Lane and titled "The Loss of Happiness in Market Democracies" has shown that "as material prosperity increases, the gap between income and satisfaction with life seems to be widening ... level of income has almost nothing to do with happiness."

The study found that in "1950 approximately 60% of people described themselves as 'happy.' Although that figure has not changed much over the years, the percentage of people describing themselves as 'very happy' has declined from 7.5% in 1950 to about 6% today."[8] Even more disturbing is the dramatic increase of depression. Whereas bipolar depression is recognized as a physical illness and can be treated with medication, unipolar depression is not. Unipolar depression is thought to arise from something "in our own minds" or in society itself. Whatever the cause, "unipolar depression just keeps rising in incidence, *with no end in sight.*"[9]

What could be the factor—across the whole population—that is "in our minds" or in "society" to cause us to be less happy? The study does come to a conclusion about what makes us happiest, and in the process, it points to a possible cause of our unhappiness. More than any other element, Professor Lane reports, "Close relationships, rather than money [or material goods], are the key to happiness."[10]

Thus, when all the philosophers have had their say, it appears that the connectedness among and between individuals and the mutual empathy it engenders is the most powerful determinant of happiness. This seems to apply even more convincingly to people living with Parkinson's or any chronic illness. Thus, what we often refer to as our "support system" is not just important. It is crucial. It is our best chance of creating a happy state of being for ourselves.

It is worth noting that Homer—without benefit of Platonic or Aristotelean theories or for that matter, the Institute of Social Policy Studies research—has Odysseus extending his best hopes for a young princess's happiness by wishing her "no greater gift in the world" than marriage and a home and harmony and no greater source of joy than "two hearts that work as one."

Admittedly, everything is more difficult with Parkinson's, which, of course, includes maintaining social connectedness. But there is no denying that we *feel* better after a loved one calls or after having lunch with a friend or after seeing a doctor who might not be able to give us anything more than encouragement or after watching children at play. We come back again to the power of the little moments in life that remain accessible to us all. "The great events in life often leave one unmoved," Oscar Wilde wrote. "They pass out of consciousness, and when one thinks of them, become unreal ... But the little things, the things of no moment remain with us.

In some ivory cell the brain stores the most delicate, the most fleeting impressions."[11] Most of those moments are not solitary.

The Western literary canon offers a vast and textured examination of what happens when people pursuing their idea of happiness get it wrong and when people get it right. It is the story of humanity in the aggregate as well as a singular narrative that can apply to any one of us. We all seek happiness. Some have a harder time of it than others because of either circumstance or personal failings. They glimpse happiness rarely or not at all. Others have the knack, or maybe they are just lucky. It is no accident that the derivation of the word *happy* comes from the Old Norse word *happ*, meaning "good luck." Perhaps in our cultural subconscious or from whatever human sensibility gives rise to language, we intuitively grasp the connection between luck and happiness.

In a story called "The Rocking-Horse Winner," D. H. Lawrence captures with perfect pitch our elemental longing for genuine happiness and our sad inadequacy in pursuing it successfully.

The story takes place in England in the early part of the twentieth century and concerns a middle-class family living beyond their means.[12] The mother detests her life and feels her children were "thrust upon her." "When her children were present, she always felt the centre of her heart go hard… she knew at the centre of her heart was a hard little place that could not feel love, no, not for anybody." She knew this to be true, and so did her children. "They read it in each other's eyes." The father, unsuccessful in business, is hardly a presence. Their stressed financial position was such that an oppressive feeling pervaded the home so much so that "the house came to be haunted by the unspoken phrase: *There must be more money! There must be more money!* The children could hear it all the time, though nobody said it aloud." In a conversation with his mother, Paul hears her say that his father is unlucky. When you're lucky, you have plenty of money.

To ease the family's burden and to earn his mother's love, Paul bets on horse races, unbeknownst to his mother. Inexplicably, as if by magic, he is able to pick winners almost each time he rides his toy rocking horse. He earns thousands of pounds and arranges for the money to be given to his mother anonymously. But in a climactic moment, he falls off the rocking horse and dies. His last *pick* wins £70,000. He has rescued the family's fortunes, but all for naught. His mother still cannot love him, even in death. The money he won was not nearly sufficient to secure his mother's affections or happiness or his family's intimacy. In the final analysis, happiness is not a function of wealth or even well-being but of emotional fulfillment among the people who count in our lives. And that cannot be bought.

The point here is not to idealize social relationships. We all know how destructive they can sometimes be, and there certainly is truth in Tolstoy's famous opening line of *Anna Karenina*. "Happy families are all alike; every unhappy family is unhappy in its own way."[13] But despite the many imperfections of family, friends, and lovers, we are unlikely to find happiness alone or in the externals of our lives. If it is to be found at all, it is somewhere in the space between us. Tolstoy does not have the final word on this. No one really does, but Yeats comes very close.

> What do we know but that we face
> One another in this place?[14]

CHAPTER 15

Death

Eugene Delacroix, *"Hamlet and Horatio in the Cemetery"*, Erich Lessing/ Art Resource. NY

And the dead tree gives no shelter, the cricket no relief,
And the dry stone no sound of water. Only
There is shadow under this red rock,

(Come under the shadow of this red rock),
And I will show you something different from either
Your shadow at morning striding behind you
Or your shadow at evening rising to meet you;
I will show you fear in a handful of dust."

—T. S. Eliot, *The Waste Land*[1]

In book 16 of *The Iliad*, Sarpedon, the son of Zeus and a mortal woman, lies wounded and dying on the battlefield of Troy. Zeus aches to save his son's life, but his wife, the goddess Hera, reminds him that Sarpedon's doom was sealed when he was born of a human mother. Zeus does not interfere. Death is a certainty for mortals. "No one," wrote Auden, "is ever spared except in dreams."[2]

The ancient Greeks and Egyptians believed in an afterlife. In the case of the Greeks, it was a netherworld of restless, unquiet shades. Although Homer makes reference to Elysium, a paradise of sorts for the privileged few, the dark, inhospitable underworld of Hades was the terminus for virtually everyone else.[3] The Egyptians, especially those of the earlier kingdoms, had a more elaborate and developed concept of the afterlife, one that involved the transfiguration of the dead into a higher-level free-ranging spirit called *ba*, which found unity with the cosmos.[4]

Christianity introduced a far more specific covenant relative to both the requirements for experiencing an afterlife and the nature of it.

> Verily, verily, I say unto to you, He that heareth my word, and believeth on him that sent me, hath everlasting life, and shall not come into condemnation; but is passed from death unto life.

> Verily, verily I say unto to you, The hour is coming, and now is, when the dead shall hear the voice of the Son of God: and they that hear shall live.

—*The Holy Bible*, John[5]

There are, of course, innumerable belief systems that address the nature of death and its aftermath, if indeed they account for an aftermath. Islam envisions paradise and hell, Hinduism a reincarnation, Buddhism a series of transitional stages leading to Nirvana, Taoism reversion to nonbeing as the complement to being, and Judaism to a vague sort of heaven or "world to come."

The obvious additional option is to imagine death as the end of everything. In his most unsentimental voice, Vladimir Nabakov expresses it this way:

> The cradle rocks above an abyss, and common sense tells us that our existence is but a brief crack of light between two eternities of darkness. Although the two are identical twins, man, as a rule, views the prenatal abyss with more calm than the one he's heading for.

> —Vladimir Nabakov, *Speak, Memory*[6]

Never mind that Nabakov ignores the fact that he is positing a belief system of his own (whose "common sense" is he referring to?), Nabakov nevertheless articulates a decidedly nonspiritual vision in which life is all there is and death marks the end of existence.

At some point after being diagnosed with Parkinson's disease, it seems natural that thoughts of death would arise. While every adult acknowledges the inevitability of death on an intellectual level, one's relative youth, good health, and feeling of well-being mitigate against sensing its nearness. Barring accidents, a healthy adult might live to who knows what age? Thoughts of death are easily fended off.

Once a serious illness is introduced into the mix, however, death is no longer theoretical or distant. It is suddenly a part of the calculus of one's life. Death becomes real and proximate. Some people respond by becoming religious, others by becoming irreligious, and still others by becoming depressed or confused. And some may even become indifferent. There are no silver bullets to this dilemma as each of us must find our own way toward an accommodation of reality. Other options are available to us. Denial or delusion are favorites among human beings in distress. Dr. Johnson, one of the sages of the eighteenth-century Enlightenment, counsels us to do otherwise.

> Let us endeavor to see things as they are, and then enquire whether we ought to complain. Whether to see life as it is, will give us much consolation, I know not; but the consolation that is drawn from truth, if any there be, is solid and durable: that which may be derived from error, must be, like its original, fallacious and fugitive.
>
> —Samuel Johnson, *Letter to Bennet Langton*[7]

Among the many imperfect options available to us upon diagnosis of serious illness, facing the truth seems the least imperfect, even taking into account T. S. Eliot when he says, "Human kind cannot bear very much reality."[8] And if close attention is paid, a simple truth stubbornly reaffirms itself in life as in literature, namely *understanding what we can control and accepting what we cannot*. That may be as wise as human beings can get in this life.

Harold Bloom asserts that Hamlet is far smarter than everybody else in *Hamlet* and smarter than anyone in its audience.[9] And so it may well be. In act 5, Hamlet is speaking with his friend Horatio and awaiting the arrival of his detested uncle, King Claudius, his mother, Queen Gertrude, Laertes, and others. In the following passage, Hamlet ostensibly is referring to the impending confrontation, but he is actually speaking of death itself:

> [Hamlet]: There is a special providence in the fall of a sparrow.
> If it be [now], 'tis not to come; if it be not to come, it will be now;
> If it be not now, yet it [will] come—the readiness is all. Since no
> Man of aught he leaves, knows what is't to leave betimes, let be.[10]

The end of our lives is inescapable, whether it comes sooner or later. To "let be" is to embrace a level of understanding and acceptance that brings us resolution and peace. There is a remarkable passage, for example, written by a remarkable man—Marcus Aurelius, emperor of Rome, in his *Meditations*. Marcus Aurelius was a brilliant and benevolent leader who ruled Rome for a period in the second century AD. His book is a compilation of his personal philosophy and has been regarded for two hundred centuries as a unique repository of wisdom. As for the issue of readiness for death, he had this to say:

> All the blessings which you pray to obtain hereafter could be yours today, if you did not deny them to yourself. You have only to have done with the past altogether, commit the future to providence, and seek to direct the present hour aright into the path of holiness and justice; holiness, by a loving acceptance of your personal lot, since Nature produced it for you and you for it: justice, in your speech by a frank and straightforward truthfulness, and in your acts by a respect for law and every man's rights. Allow yourself, too, no hindrance from the malice, misconceptions or slanders of others, nor yet from any sensations this fleshy frame may feel; its afflicted part will look to itself. The hour for your departure draws near; if you will but forget all else and pay sole regard to the helmsman of your soul and the divine spark within you—if you will but exchange your fear of failing even to begin it on nature's true principles—you can become a man, worthy of the universe that gave you birth, instead of a stranger in your own homeland, bewildered by each day's happenings as though by wonders unlooked for, and ever hanging upon this one or the next.

—Marcus Aurelius, *Meditations*[11]

Marcus Aurelius was a stoic and pantheistic philosopher. He viewed the individual as capable of shaping his destiny and the universe as having been created by a divine power that is manifest in all things. For Marcus Aurelius, death is a return to and reunification of the individual with all things, and in some respects, this echoes the Judeo-Christian view that "all go unto one place; all are of the dust and all turn to dust again."[12]

The humanistic philosophy embodied by Marcus Aurelius as well as organized religion and spiritualism of almost any kind all attempt to accommodate death as part of the natural order of things. It could hardly be otherwise. In the countless millennia before the twentieth century, mankind has been at the mercy of natural forces with few defenses available against them. The development of the germ theory of disease in the late nineteenth century by Louis Pasteur and Robert Koch was perhaps the single most significant finding in medical science since the time of Hippocrates's snake pits and healing baths at the Asklepion in the fourth century BC. Joseph Lister's seemingly simple recognition in the 1860's of the importance of antiseptic surgery reduced the death rate in his surgical procedures to 15 percent from 49 percent.[13] Prior to these advances, death had been a frequent and familiar part of life—at birth, in childhood, in the flower of youth, and in middle age. Since the dawn of human history, life for the overwhelming majority of people was, as Thomas Hobbes famously declared, "nasty, brutish and short."

Hobbes's bleak view has become an unacceptable prospect for any human being in the contemporary mind-set, which holds that everyone has a right to a full and happy life and that our task as a society is to defeat poverty and disease. This bias is aggressively at odds with the very notion of the *naturalness* of death. Death has evolved from being viewed as a necessary part of eternal cycles to being regarded as a flaw in the human genome, a defect in the genetic program, a perverse technical configuration that can eventually be reengineered. Death has been exposed as a molecular error message.

Our self-evident cultural obsession with youth—aimed at overcoming aging—has now evolved into an obsession with overcoming death itself. Consider the following opening to science journalist and author Ronald

Bailey's provocatively titled book *Liberation Biology: The Scientific and Moral Case for the Biotech Revolution,*

By the end of the 21ˢᵗ century, the typical American may attend a family reunion in which five generations are playing together. And great-great-great grandma, at 150 years old, will be as vital, with muscle tone as firm and supple, skin as elastic and glowing, as the thirty-year-old great-great-grandson with whom she's playing touch football.[14]

While the search for immortality is as old as mankind, we are now immersed so thoroughly in an environment of advancing technology and medical science that it is increasingly difficult for us to regard death with equanimity. It is being substantially forestalled. Why could it not eventually be vanquished? Death is no longer a part of the endlessly repeated cycle of cosmic order applying alike to a flower and a galaxy. It has become a conquerable frontier.

Thus, in a climate of limitless technological possibilities, those of us in the last generations before this great (or dubious) achievement might understandably feel luckless for having to face death (it might now be imagined) *unnecessarily*. We might be excused, too, if we feel less resigned to it or less philosophical about it than our forebears. Ironically, our ability to stay alive longer and the prospect of extending life indefinitely has not been comforting but deeply troubling. Daniel Callahan, cofounder for the Hastings Center, a bioethics think tank, has baldly declared, "There is no known social good coming from the conquest of death."[15] It is difficult to imagine Marcus Aurelius disagreeing with Dr. Callahan.

The opposing forces of what promises to become perhaps the most consequential moral and ethical controversy in human history are even now beginning to gather. On one side are the "bio conservatives" who generally oppose human reproductive cloning and stem cell research and who view the area of biotechnology as essentially illegitimate and immoral. Francis Fukuyama, the historian, has pejoratively dubbed this coming era as "post humanity."[16] On the other side of the argument are those who hold, as Ronald Bailey does, that manipulation of science to meet human needs and desires is wholly legitimate. If the basis for opposing human reproductive cloning and biotechnology is that it seeks to "liberate the human race from its biological constraints and limitations," Bailey argues that human history has always been about liberating us from our physical limitations. When man first used a stone or stick to kill for food, he was compensating for his limitation of speed and strength.[17] For Bailey, the case against the morality of biotechnology advancement is unconvincing.

The fact of the matter is that the philosophical and ethical arguments on this issue must be made in the real context of millions of people suffering concrete illnesses and "biological limitations." Yet we have to expect that we will remain for the foreseeable future in an in-between world of unprecedented promise in biotechnology on the one hand and resistance to its unfettered advance on the other. This demands grace in the "loving acceptance of our personal lot," as Marcus Aurelius counsels, but unavoidably includes disappointment that not enough is being done or that the work is being done too slowly. We are being teased by history and destiny.

Like it or not, we are still in Marcus Aurelius' s "human" rather than Fukuyama's "post human" world. And as we are here, the old truths abide. Ours is the lot that humanity has had from the beginning. Readiness is still all. But with it comes *hope*, which is decidedly human, as opposed to *certainty*, which is not yet ours.

In 2004, Seamus Heaney eulogized the death of fellow poet Czeslaw Milosz with a poem titled "What Passed at Colonus." Heaney captures the extraordinary grace with which Milosz faced his death and—following a lifetime of extraordinary work—the effect his passing had on Heaney and Milosz's children. Heaney pays tribute to an enviable life and a dignified death free of contemporary philosophical complications and vexations.

> His instruction calmed us, his company and voice
> Were like high tidings in the summer trees,
> Except this time he turned and left us.
> … And when all was done, and the daughters waiting,

There came a noise like waters rising fast
Far underground, then a low blast and rush
As if some holy name were breathed on air,
A sound that when they heard it made the girls
Cry out, and made blind Oedipus
Gather them in his arms, "My children," he said—
And the rest of us felt that we were his then too—
"Today is the day that ends your father's life.
The burden I have been to myself and you
Is lifted. And yet it was eased by love.

Now you must do without me and relearn
The meaning of that word by remembering."
… No god had galloped
His thunder chariot, no hurricane
Had swept the hill. Call me mad if you like,
Or gullible, but that man surely went
In step with a guide he trusted down to where
Light has gone out but the door stands open."

—Seamus Heaney, from "What Passed at Colonus"[18]

CHAPTER 16

Heaven and Hell

Gustave Dore, "***Dante and Virgil at the Entrance to Hell***", bpk, Berlin, Art Resource, NY

And whosoever shall offend one of these little ones that believe in me, it is better for him that a millstone were hanged about his neck, and he were cast out to sea.

And if thy hand offend thee, cut it off; it is better for thee to enter into life maimed, than having two hands to go into hell, into the fire that never shall be quenched.

Where their worm dieth not and the fire is not quenched.

And if thy foot offend thee cut it off: it is better for thee to enter halt into life than having two feet to be cast into hell, into the fire that never shall be quenched:

Where their worm dieth not and the fire is not quenched.

And if thy eye offend thee pluck it out; it is better for thee to enter into the kingdom of God with one eye, than having two eyes to be cast into hell fire;

Where their worm dieth not and the fire is not quenched.

For everyone shall be salted with fire and every sacrifice shall be salted with salt.

—The Holy Bible, Mark[1]

The unwelcome arrival of a serious illness invariably raises the specter of death, and reflecting upon death unavoidably leads to at least some consideration of the hereafter. Seamus Heaney's eulogy (cited in the last chapter) moves from the acknowledgment of death to thoughts of an existence beyond it, to a place "where light has gone out but the door stands open."[2] And if we come to believe that the hereafter does exist—that there is a there *there*—a new set of questions arises. Is there a heaven and hell? If so, what are they like? And of course, where am I headed?

As for the question of God's existence, one would have expected broad agreement with Nietzsche, who at the dawn of the twentieth century pronounced God dead. The century that unfolded contained catastrophes in such number and magnitude as to threaten the survival of humanity. Would a benevolent God stand by with folded arms? Fifty million to a hundred million died in the flu pandemic of 1918–19. Stalin starved and murdered millions to pursue an ideological and political agenda. Mao's cultural revolution gave free rein to widespread public slaughter. Man could now kill on an unimaginable scale, and he did. And man continued to exhibit the primal venality and lust for power and wealth that has marred his soul from the start. Yet no god rose to stay man's hand at Gallipoli; at Auschwitz or Berkinau; at Nanking, Hiroshima, or Phnom Penh; or at countless other places of human misery and death. Age-old ruinous diseases still afflict us and have yielded little ground despite our prayers and potions.

In the midst of this malignant chaos science and technology emerged as new gods offering revelation through reason rather than faith. Man could fly not by virtue of prayer but by native ingenuity. He could heal illnesses that had plagued mankind for millennia, work his will on molecules and atoms, and manipulate bits of protein strands that are the stuff of life itself. He discovered a calculus by which he could fix the birth date of the universe, the speed of light, and the distance to the edge of space. And he walked on the moon.

Given the century's history, why would we not conclude with Nietzsche that God is indeed dead or at the very most, utterly indifferent? In either case, what need does man have of God?

Evidently, we have a great deal of need. Americans in overwhelming numbers believe in God, the afterlife, heaven, hell, angels, and the devil. The Gallup Organization has been tracking Americans' beliefs in deities and the afterlife since 1944. It has found on a consistent basis that close to 90 percent of Americans believe in God or a universal spirit. Eighty-one percent believe heaven exists, and 77 percent describe their chances of getting there as "excellent" or "good." Somewhat fewer people—70 percent—believe in the existence of hell, but only 6 percent think their chances of arriving there are "excellent" or "good." In fact, 79 percent are certain their chances are "poor" of going to hell.[3]

In light of these findings, one might question whether the reality of our *actual* conduct is consistent with our celestial expectations. Why are we so optimistic?

These Gallup data suggest a plausible answer. Americans might be horrified about what havoc others are wreaking but seem to have rationalized their personal behavior as mostly benign and heaven-bound. We seem to have substantially *lowered* the price of entry into heaven so that the road to heaven is broad, the gate open wide. At the same time, we've *raised* the bar of misbehavior that would warrant eternal damnation. According to Gallup, most of us believe that heaven is a place "where people who had led good lives are eternally rewarded." Hell is reserved for those few of us "who led bad lives without being sorry" and "a place where they will be eternally damned."[4] It is easy to imagine Hitler or Stalin burning for eternity on a sulphurous lake, but does my atheist neighbor who volunteers for our town's recycling campaign merit the same fate? Can he be said to have led a "bad life" merely for lacking faith? Perhaps along with beer, butter, and ice cream, we've created a heaven- and hell-Lite.

If we have made heaven more accessible and reserve hell for the truly evil elite, our imaginings are a far cry from Judeo-Christian tradition. According to those traditions, perdition is frighteningly real, and our lives and eternal souls are suspended over an abyss by a slender thread. This is hell unadorned and designed by the same God that destroyed everyone save Noah and his family and razed Sodom and Gomorrah without mercy. It is precisely this God and the consequences of defying Him that were so clearly manifest one summer Sunday morning in 1741 in Enfield, Connecticut.

On that day, a preacher of the gospel named Jonathan Edwards delivered a sermon to his flock of such ferocious power and eloquence that it left a scar on the collective American soul. Edwards titled his sermon "Sinners in the Hands of an Angry God," and through it, he bequeathed to a young America a vision of hell and a wrathful God that is uncompromising, horrific, and indelible.

To Edwards, hell was not a concept but a real place of indescribable suffering, the terminus for sinners who will suffer God's eternal wrath. (Such was the promise made in Revelation 21:8, which says, "But the fearful, and unbelieving ... shall have their part in the lake which burneth with fire and brimstone.") There was no doubt in his mind, he declaimed, that some seated in the pews that very day would be cast into the abyss before the year was out. Yet until the moment of death, one can choose to be born again. But rejecting that choice seals one's fate for eternity and leads to certain perdition. His congregants must have been spellbound as Edwards admonished them without restraint or compassion from his pulpit.

> Men are held in the hand of God, over the pit of hell; they have deserved the fiery pit, and are already sentenced to it; and God is dreadfully provoked, his anger is as great towards them as to those who are actually suffering the executions of the fierceness of his wrath ... the devil is waiting for them, hell is gaping for them, the flames gather and flash about them, and would fain lay hold on them and swallow them up; the fire pent up in their own hearts is struggling to break out ... That world of misery, that lake of burning brimstone, is extended abroad under you. There is the dreadful pit of the glowing flames of the wrath of God; there is hell's wide gaping mouth open; and you have nothing to stand upon, nor anything to take hold of; there is nothing between you and hell but air: it is only the power and mere pleasure of God that holds you up.

> —Jonathan Edwards, "Sinners in the Hands of an Angry God"[5]

Edwards's portrayal of hell not only as a place of external torment but as a place of human drama is as much inspired by John Milton as by the Bible. In book 1 of *Paradise Lost*, Milton tells of Lucifer's and his angels' rebellion against God, which resulted in their being cast out of heaven by Him and condemned to hell. "Bottomless perdition, there to dwell/ In adamantine chains and penal fire."[6] "Confounded though immortal," Lucifer scans with a fallen angel's eyes the nature of the place to which he's been condemned.

> At once, as far as Angels ken, he views
> The dismal situation waste and wild;
> A dungeon horrible on all sides round,
> As one great furnace flamed; yet from those flames
> No light, but darkness visible
> Served only to discover sights of woe,
> Regions of sorrow, doleful shades, where peace
> And rest can never dwell, hope never comes
> That comes to all, but torture without end
> Still urges, and a fiery deluge, fed
> With ever-burning sulphur consumed.
>
> —John Milton, *Paradise Lost*[7]

Lucifer (or Satan) is arguably the hero of *Paradise Lost*. He rebelled against God, whom he considered an oppressor, and would rather be punished for eternity in hell than bend to His will. Satan's star power has not been diminished since *Paradise Lost* was published in 1667. The same Gallup poll showing that close to 90 percent of us believe in the existence of God finds that 78 percent of us believe in angels and 70 percent of us believe in the devil. What is curious about both numbers is that they have been rising but that belief in the devil has been trending upward more dramatically. In 1990, only 55 percent of adult Americans believed in the devil. By 2004, the number rose to 70 percent.[8]

No doubt Lucifer's recent resurgence has much to do with the rise of terrorism, 9/11, and the perceived deterioration of important social and cultural institutions like the government and the financial system and perhaps a perceived increase also in bellicosity among nations. And yet there has been no corresponding decline in the belief in God or angels. Seventy-eight percent of Americans believe in angels (the kind with wings) who are at the service of God. Perhaps a showdown is brewing. Perhaps the apocalypse is not distant. Yet there is some consolation in all of these data points. We persist in our conviction that a divinity exists and that He is on the side of the good.

Any reflection on the nature of heaven and hell—at least from a Western perspective—is incomplete without consideration of Dante Alighieri's *Divine Comedy*. Dante's masterpiece, in which he describes in three books his visit to hell ("The Inferno"), purgatory ("The Purgatorio"), and paradise ("The Paradiso"), is among the most celebrated literary works ever written. Like the Bible and *Paradise Lost*, it has had a major role in constructing through incomparable poetry a vision of the afterlife in the Western mind.

After leading a dissolute life, Dante finds himself in a "dark wood" where he encounters the spirit of Virgil, the great Roman poet of *The Aeneid*. Virgil offers to guide him through hell and purgatory. However, since he lived before Christ and therefore has not been baptized, Virgil is prohibited from entering heaven. Another guide, beautiful and perfect, will take Dante to heaven and closer to the "King of Time." That guide will be Beatrice, the unrequited love of Dante's life.

Unlike Jonathan Edwards and even the Bible, Dante recognizes degrees of sin and maps the geography of hell with exactitude. An illustration follows: [9]

Dante's Hell

Sandro Botticelli, *"Map of Hell"*, bpk, Berlin/Art Resource, NY

In the context of our contemporary world, there is something remarkably insightful and prescient in Dante's notion that traitors and perpetrators merit sentencing to the deepest part of hell, specifically the Ninth Circle. We have seen the human price that has been paid as a result of fraud in the world financial system and the betrayal of fiscal responsibility and trust. The Ninth Circle, too, is where Satan, the avatar of evil, has been condemned for his treasonous revolt against God. There he will abide for eternity—voiceless, beastly, and chest-deep in a fiery lake.

There are notable departures in *The Divine Comedy* from the Bible, Christian orthodoxy, and certainly Milton. Satan is no less evil in "The Inferno" than in the Bible, but he is not as much of a free agent and not nearly as human. His domain is limited to the Ninth Circle of hell, where he is joined by the most odious sinners. By way of contrast, in the Old Testament and *Paradise Lost*, Satan is much like a prince—literally a fallen prince—cunning and articulate and conducting an ongoing battle against the Father for the soul of man. In the book of Job (1:7), God summons Satan and asks where he has been, and the devil answers, "From going to and fro in the earth, and from walking up and down in it." God asks if Satan knows of Job, His faithful and righteous servant. Satan responds by asking rhetorically, "Why wouldn't Job be faithful and righteous?" After all, God has given him everything a man could possibly want. Satan is the archetypal miscreant son to the tenth power, forever sowing mischief and rebellion against the Patriarch.

Thus, it is not only the existence of evil that threatens man but also the cleverness and power of Lucifer as he demonstrates in the garden of Eden, the book of Job, the garden of Gethsemane, and elsewhere in the Bible. Dante's Satan is virtually entombed; his battle against God has been lost. The fate of man—and whether he chooses good or evil—is not subject to active interference by the devil but based solely on man's personal choices.

When 70 percent of Americans report, as they do to the Gallup pollsters, that the devil "is something I believe in," there is no telling what each person actually means. Individual impressions may represent some amalgam of church doctrine, the Bible, Milton, Dante, even Goethe's *Faust*, or countless Hollywood characterizations, all of which have left their mark on the general culture. Yet one thing is certain. However the devil is perceived, he is by definition the antithesis of a benevolent God, and a belief in the devil presumes belief in his opposite number and a life beyond the temporal. Michael Cunningham captures a contemporary sense of the devil in his novel, *The Hours*.

> The devil is a headache; the devil is a voice inside a wall; the devil is a fin breaking through dark waves. The devil is the brief, twittering nothing that was the thrush's life. The devil sucks all the beauty out of the world, all the hope, and what remains when the devil has finished is a realm of the living dead—joyless, suffocating … For the devil is many things but he is not petty, not sentimental; he seethes with a lethal, intolerable truth.
>
> —Michael Cunningham, *The Hours*[10]

Cunningham makes the point that the devil and evil by extension is everywhere, and the devil himself is a potent agent of evil. At the same time, the "intolerable truth" he possesses is that we are perennially susceptible to his seductive powers. This is Milton's devil—a free agent of evil who nonetheless demands admiration as he declares to his fallen minions that "the mind is its own place, and in itself/Can make a Heaven of Hell, a Hell of Heaven."[11]

Ironically, when the Archangel Michael shows Adam and Eve the future of mankind before escorting them out of Eden, he reassures them in virtually the same way as Satan reassured himself. He tells Adam that although he's been cast out of Eden, he might find a "paradise within thee, happier far."[12] This is an extraordinary declaration of independence and assertion of man's freedom and the promise of redemption.

Milton portrays a humanized and even admirable Satan throughout *Paradise Lost* (so much so that some scholars have argued that Milton's intent was not, as he claimed, "to justify the ways of God to men" but rather to expose His injustice).

At the turn of the century, an anonymous writer in the New York Times reflected on the differences between Dante's and Milton's images of heaven. Milton described it in human terms as familiar earthly terrain divinely perfected. It is a place suffused with the scent of ambrosia, where the sun rises and sets, fruit trees and nectar abound, rivers flow, the sky arches above, and gentle breezes blow. Dante, on the other hand, imagines a heaven far more mystical "passing from glory to glory in ascending brightness, with divine visions that come and go like stars in a cloudy night, and attended by the music of the spheres. These are the two extremes, between which lesser poets paint and plant their Edens."[13]

We are the lesser poets. We are beset with suffering—all of us, ill and well alike. Can we be faulted for asking in our private ways, "Can this be all of it? Does it end here, now, and melt into nothingness?" Most of us say no and turn away to draw a promise from the deep well of doctrine and art, folklore and tradition, dreams and faith, of something more. And like Dante, we hear—faintly but surely—the music of the spheres.

Vincent van Gogh, "*The Starry Night*", The Metropolitan Museum of Art/Art Resource, NY

CHAPTER 17

Freedom, Fate, and Chance

Ludwig Ferdinand Graf, "*The Judgment of Paris*",
Erich Lessing/Art Resource, NY

Achilles: Mother tells me,
The immortal goddess Thetis with her glistening feet,

122

That two fates bear me on to the day of death.
If I hold out here and I lay siege to Troy,
My journey home is gone, but my glory never dies.
If I voyage back to the fatherland I love,
My pride, my glory dies…
True, but the life that's left me will be long.
The stroke of death will not come on me quickly.

—Homer, *The Iliad*[1]

The journey that is one's life—its central narrative, the direction it takes, the turns it makes, and the end it meets—plays out as a drama whose animating forces are almost never clear. The life we lead may be governed by our own choices or fate or chance, but we can never be sure of the precise role of each.

We receive a diagnosis of Parkinson's disease, for example. Has that been in the cards all along? Did we have nothing to do with it, or did we make choices along the road that led to it? If those choices had not been made, would there have been a different outcome? Once having been made, could they have been unmade? And most nettlesome of all questions, was that diagnosis the work of an invisible hand that long ago determined the stations of our journey?

Personal freedom, fate, and chance have been perennial themes in the literature and culture of the West. Judeo-Christian theology for the most part asserts that free will exists even though God already knows the past, the present, and all things to come. "I am Alpha and Omega, the beginning and the ending, saith the Lord, which is, and which was, and which is to come, the Almighty."[2]

The apparent contradiction in the coexistence of God's foreknowledge and free will was no contradiction at all to St. Augustine. Nor is it today to the faithful. Even though God knows the choice Eve will make before she makes it, Eve is nevertheless free to say no. She freely chose to say yes. The same foundational belief is expressed by Job even after he suffers unimaginable pain and loss. "Let me alone that I may speak, and let come on me what will … Though He slay me yet will I trust in Him: but I will maintain mine own ways before Him."[3]

Most contemporary Judeo-Christian belief aligns with St. Augustine's view that free will exists *even though* God knows beforehand what choices will be made. How can this be? St. Augustine explains it this way:

> We do not deny God's foreknowledge of all things future, and yet we do will what we will. Since God has foreknowledge of our will, its future will be such as he foreknows it. It will be a will precisely because he foreknows it as a will, and it could not be a will if it were not in our power. Hence God also has foreknowledge of our power over it. The power, then, is not taken from me because of his foreknowledge, since this power will be mine all the more certainly because of the infallible knowledge of Him who foreknew that I would have it.
>
> —St. Augustine, *De Libero Arbitrio*[4]

This reasoning also reflects the contention that our choices are not *actually* true until they happen. Since God transcends time and is aware of all things past, present, and future (at once the Alpha and Omega), He does not so much *predict* our choices as much as embody the truth of them. As God embodies perfect truth and knows that our will is free, it must therefore be true that it is free.

Yet without some leap of faith, St. Augustine's argument may still not satisfy. There are those who believe that free will is an illusion in the context of an all-knowing God. Isn't Eve *compelled* to eat the apple because God has foreknowledge of it and He cannot be wrong? Therefore, isn't the world and everything in it an extension of God's will while we are merely acting out our predetermined roles in fulfilling His plan? If Eve chooses to resist Satan's temptations, God would have been wrong, and if He were wrong, He would not be God.

The struggle to reconcile seemingly irreconcilable opposites of freedom on the one hand and determinism or fatalism on the other continues in our private thoughts and in society at large.

> In any civilization which makes its place in its thoughts for free will (and therefore individual responsibility) and pattern (and therefore overall meaning), the two concepts—fixed and free—exist uneasily cheek by jowl. The only escape from this logical contradiction is the prison of rigid determinism, a pattern fixed from the beginning and not subject to change, or on the other hand, the complete freedom and meaningless anarchy of an unpredictable universe.

—Bernard Knox, "Introduction" *to The Odyssey*[5]

When we are diagnosed with Parkinson's or any other serious illness, the *reconciliation* we reach affects the quality of our lives. If we tend toward a fatalistic or deterministic view, we might adopt patterns of behavior and coping mechanisms consistent with that view. If we were convinced that we exist in an anarchic, random, and arbitrary universe, we might act otherwise. Or believing in our *agency* or freedom, we would pursue yet different paths.

"Fixed vs. Free," as Knox terms it so directly, was one of the earliest subjects to be explored in the classic dramas of West. A prophecy is made, and a fated point is fixed in the future. The prophecy then becomes the center of gravity of the play. Outcomes involving life or death, glory or disgrace, moral order or moral chaos all hang in the balance. Matters move toward an irresistible climax, and finally, an order of sorts is affirmed as the consequences of one man's character flaws play out while our common humanity is revealed ... for better or worse.

In one case, the prophecy is horrific. It is foretold in Sophocles' *Oedipus the King* that Oedipus, the infant son of King Laius of Thebes and Queen Jocasta, will grow up to kill his father and marry his mother. Moral order and a kingdom threatened, events must now move to meet a fixed destiny … or must they? Can they do otherwise? Is the prophecy true, or is it a deception? Can it be averted?

It is difficult to ignore the parallel between this classical dramatic framework and the sudden introduction of serious illness into our lives. The difference between a prediction made in the fifth century BC in Athens that is called a *prophecy* and a prediction made in in the twenty-first century in Manhattan that is called a *prognosis* is science. In both instances, signs and portents are interpreted by those who specialize in such things. Many times the signs augur well, many times not. Although the distinctions between ancient prophecy and modern prognosis are obviously great, human response is not. Once the ancient prophecy or the modern prognosis is made, the question is the same. Are those involved in the outcome fixed or free? Can they be both? Can Thebes be saved? Is a prognosis mutable? Can the course of events be influenced so that the outcome is different than was foretold?

Naturally, King Laius and Jocasta are stunned but decide that they are free agents and the prophecy need not be passively accepted. Fate can be changed. Having the will to act, they do. They send the child Oedipus off to be killed by one of their servants in order to preclude any possibility of the prophecy coming to fruition. Pitying the child, the servant spares his life and gives him over to a shepherd in the countryside. There he is found and adopted by the childless king and queen of Corinth, Polybos and Merope. Oedipus grows up in Corinth, believing that Polybos and Merope are his biological parents. One night at a banquet, the young prince Oedipus is told by a guest that the king and queen are not his natural parents. Oedipus then consults an oracle to establish the truth or falsehood of this disturbing information, whereupon the prophecy that he will kill his father and marry his mother is told to him. The prophecy/prognosis is corroborated with devastating effect.

Oedipus leaves Corinth to ensure that there is no possibility for the prophecy to come true. On the road he quarrels with another traveler. They duel, and he slays the man, but unbeknownst to Oedipus, this man is King Laius himself. Oedipus continues his journey to Corinth, and on the way he solves the riddle of the Sphinx, thereby freeing Thebes from the grips of a plague. Welcomed in Thebes as a hero of obvious royal lineage, Oedipus is made king, marries the newly widowed Jocasta, who becomes his queen, and soon fathers two children by her. The prophecy has been fulfilled, a fact unknown to all but the gods and to Tiresias, an old soothsayer.

All of the events up to this point are the backstory to the play. *Oedipus the King* actually opens as Thebes again is suffering under a plague, and the gods declare that it will lift only when the murderer of King Laius is found. Oedipus takes it upon himself to find him.

The irony, of course, is that up to this point, the key players have done everything possible to negate the prophecy originally told to Laius and Jocasta and later to Oedipus himself. All efforts have been to no avail. In fact, deciding to send the child away and having him killed only advances the possibility of the fated outcome by keeping Oedipus ignorant of the identity of his true parents. Oedipus leaves Corinth to escape the prophecy and instead draws nearer to it. And now—though he does not know it—ignorance of the truth remains his last refuge.

But yet in his overweening pride to know all, control all, he determines to uncover the truth regardless of its consequences. He eventually does, and so great is his revulsion, so consuming is his remorse that he tears the brooches from Jocasta's robe and puts out his eyes. Blindness, now that the truth is clear, is what he chooses rather than enduring the sight of his debasement.

> What I have done here was best done—don't tell me
> Otherwise, do not give me further counsel.
> I do not know with what eyes I could look
> Upon my father when I die and go under the earth, nor
> yet my wretched mother—
> Would the sight of my children, bred as mine are,
> gladden me?
> No, not these eyes, ever.

> —Sophocles, *Oedipus the King*[6]

"Do not seek to be master of everything," declares Creon, Jocasta's brother, near the close of the play—not master of fate or of truth or even of every turn in your life. The chorus ends on a doleful note for the man fallen from greatness.

> You that live in my ancestral Thebes, behold this
> Oedipus—
> Him who knew the famous riddles and was a man most
> masterful;
> Not a citizen who did not look with envy on his lot—
> See him now and see the breakers of misfortune
> swallow him!
> Look upon that last day always. Count no mortal happy till
> He has passed the final limit of his life secure from pain.[7]

In Oedipus's case, fate proved immutable, truth unbearable, and free will the unknowing servant of destiny.

And what about us? What about the prophecies about us? A prognosis is pronounced by a sage. Some of us hasten to pray others to rake the web for information. Some do little but rage at the moon, and others do little but despair. How much truth do we need to have? How much free will do we need to exercise, and how little of destiny are we willing to accept? Whom or what must we control to ease a restive mind, and have we reconciled the things of real consequence in our lives? What solace do we find in sight, and in sightlessness?

Absent the *absolute certainty* that a perfect God exists and that His will is expressed in prophecy and prognosis, no one can know whether our will is free or not, whether an outcome is predetermined, or whether we can change an outcome that we can never even be sure will materialize. It turns out that the question of free or fixed is moot. It is a trick question. The answer can be neither true nor false. The only issue is whether we decide to act *as if* we are free or to act *as if* we are fated, and we can hope that we do so wisely.

CHAPTER 18

Hope

Eugene Burnand, *"St. Peter and John Running to Christ's Tomb on the Morning of the Resurrection"*, Erich Lessing/Art Resource, NY

Hope is the thing with feathers
That perches in the soul,
And sings the tune without the words,
And never stops at all,

And sweetest in the gale is heard;
And sore must be the storm
That could abash the little bird
That kept so many warm.

I've heard it in the chillest land,
And on the strangest sea;

> Yet, never, in extremity,
> It asked a crumb of me.

—Emily Dickinson, *Hope*[1]

As science tells it, only human beings among all living things can hope. We have the unique ability to imagine two time frames at once—the present and the future, what is and what might be. Hope is the state of mind that is suspended somewhere between utter impossibility at one extreme and absolute certainty on the other. It is our last firewall against despair. One day things will be better. Violence will cease. Our grandchildren will live well. A cure will be found. We are usually not at a loss for hopes. Most of us carry a satchel-full of hope for ourselves, our loved ones, our community, the nation, and the world.

Sometimes there is no accounting for the resiliency of hope. We could hardly imagine, for example, a place on earth more thoroughly devoid of hope than the Buchenwald prison camp just prior to its liberation. As in other camps, mass killings were accelerated by the Nazis near the end of the war in a frantic effort to conceal evidence of their crimes. Prisoners continued to be beaten, starved, and overworked until their time came to be gassed, a fate they faced each day until finally it came to meet them.

As it happens, Dr. Karl Menninger, the eminent American psychiatrist, entered Buchenwald the day after it was liberated by American troops. In a speech to the American Psychiatric Association in 1959, Dr. Menninger related what he had seen.

> The doctors [at Buchenwald], prisoners along with all the others, had followed the same routines of 4:00AM rising, shivering roll calls, daylong drudgery on the Autobahn, shivering roll calls again, and finally a cold bowl of thin soup …
>
> But now comes the surprise. At night, when the other prisoners were asleep, these thin, hungry, weary doctors got up and talked. They discussed cases. They organized

a medical society. They prepared and presented papers. They made plans for improving health conditions. Then they began to smuggle in materials to make various medical instruments. And finally they built, of all things, an X-ray machine ... and used it, secretly, at night, in their efforts to ameliorate the lot of their fellow prisoners. This is what dedication to medicine and humanity could do—kept alive by hope.

—Karl Menninger, MD, "An Academic Lecture on Hope"[2]

In light of Dr. Menninger's experience and our own, Emily Dickinson's metaphor of hope as "the thing with feathers/ that perches in the soul" might seem to come up short. Hope doesn't feel feathery but fierce—more like a battle cry than a melody, a hawk rather than a songbird. Menninger's muscular description of hope may come closer to its essence as "a kind of relentless pursuit of resolution and freedom."[3]

Hope is the indispensable American value so much so that lacking in hope seems un-American. Jimmy Carter lost his presidency in large part because of his so-called "malaise speech" delivered on July 15, 1979. While never mentioning the term *malaise,* Carter admonished Americans for their material excesses and had the temerity to warn us of limits even to America's growth—limits, in other words, to the American dream. Today Carter's warnings might sound to many as having been prescient, but in 1979, we would have none of it. Ronald Reagan won a landslide victory as we embraced the soaring sentiments of adman Hal Riney's voice intoning, "It's morning again in America," over a montage of gauzy scenes of American industriousness and innocence. It was pure Norman Rockwell on video.

Our reaction could hardly have been otherwise. From the beginning, the US Constitution has been our instrumentality for the exercise of personal freedom and the vast continent our matchless stage set for its expression. The notion that America and growth and hope are inextricably bound resonates throughout Fitzgerald's nearly perfect American novel *The Great Gatsby*, but nowhere is the thought more grand and sweeping than here:

> For a transitory enchanted moment man must have held his breath in the presence of this continent, compelled into an aesthetic contemplation he neither understood nor desired, face to face for the last time in history with something commensurate to his capacity for wonder.
>
> —F. Scott Fitzgerald, *The Great Gatsby*[4]

It was amassing great wealth and hope for regaining his lost love of Daisy Fay that impelled Jay Gatsby. We intuitively understand Gatsby and admire him from afar. He embodied hope as a life force. It enabled him to become rich beyond dreams and drove him to hope—indeed to be convinced—that he could even recapture the past. "Can't repeat the past? Why of course you can!"[5] Gatsby declares. With hope, anything seems possible.

There are those among us who would argue against hope by pointing to the near certainty that romantic illusions come to naught. Hemingway famously wrote in *Fathers and Sons*, "All sentimental people are betrayed so many times."[6] If a hoped-for outcome does occur, the reasoning goes, having hoped for it was irrelevant. If a hoped-for outcome does not occur, having hoped for it only results in disappointment, which would have been avoided if emotional capital had not been spent on hoping.

Logically, this makes sense, but it is a deeply cynical point of view. It ignores the possibility that hoping for something might increase its chances of happening. Being hopeful might motivate us to behave in ways that give a positive outcome a greater chance of being realized, while hopelessness might have the opposite effect. And yet despite everything Gatsby did to win back Daisy, despite his relentless and lavishly decorated hope, it all ended badly.

Unreasonable hope—hope that is delusional or envisions an occurrence whose chances are so remote as to be virtually nonexistent—always injures us, say the pragmatists. When *unjustified* hopes are dashed, as they often are, we can become depressed and resentful. The problem, of course, is this: How do we know when our hopes are unjustified?

If reasonableness is the game (and in the case of hope, it is not), the best advice would seem to be embodied in the principle of the golden mean—to experience everything in moderation, even hope, and always occupy the middle ground of sensibility. Yet hope by definition abandons the middle ground as lost. There is no solace to be found there. We are afflicted. There is no cure. The middle ground is barren, and so we hope for a cure announced in tomorrow's newspaper. The middle ground is bypassed, but that is what hope is *supposed* to do. In the poet Seamus Heaney's adaptation of Sophocles's *Philoctetes: The Cure at Troy*, we are urged to raise our sights and ignore the limits.

> Human beings suffer,
> They torture one another,
> They get hurt and get hard.
> No poem or play or song
> Can fully right a wrong
> Inflicted and endured.
>
> History says, Don't hope
> On this side of the grave.
> But then, once in a lifetime
> The longed-for tidal wave
> Of justice can rise up,
> And hope and history rhyme.
>
> So hope for a great sea-change
> On the far side of revenge.
> Believe that a further shore
> Is reachable from here.
> Believe in miracles
> And cures and healing wells

—Seamus Heaney, *The Cure at Troy: A Version of Sophocles' Philoctetes*[7]

On the other side of the ledger, as mentioned earlier, is the view that if there are indeed "miracles and cures and healing wells," they will present themselves with or without our hoping for them. If they do not present themselves, hoping merely invites disappointment and spiritual hurt. Certainly, this is a risk in the case of wholly unrealistic expectations.

But some of us find that even a modest, restrained feeling of hope has slipped away. We abandon hope altogether and succumb to a darker state of mind—a state that is spiritually closer to evil than to good. In Dante's *Inferno*, the inscription "Lay Down All Hope, You That Go In By Me" appears over the gates of hell.[8] For Dante, the *absence* of hope is a part of the experience of hell, an essential aspect of its punishment, and therefore a component of evil. Conversely, the existence of hope—or perhaps more accurately, the *persistence* of hope—is a good. It keeps open the possibility of deliverance.

Although being hopeful may appear to be a purely personal issue, it is not entirely so. The inclination to be hopeful ebbs and flows with the times as well as with our personal circumstances. We can no more escape the "spirit of the times" (the infamous *zeitgeist*) than climb out of our skin. In one of the best known opening passages in English literature, Charles Dickens expresses how closely interrelated and reflexive our public and personal emotional states are.

> It was the best of times, it was the worst of times, it was the age of wisdom, it was the age of foolishness, it was the epoch of belief, it was the epoch of incredulity, it was the season of Light, it was the season of Darkness, it was the spring of hope, it was the winter of despair, we had everything before us, we had nothing before us, we were all going direct to Heaven, we were all going direct the other way—in short, the period was so far like the present period, that some its noisiest authorities insisted on its being received, for good or evil, in the superlative degree of comparison only.

> —Charles Dickens, *A Tale of Two Cities*[9]

And what of our times? Are they biased toward hopefulness or despair?

Perhaps not since the election of Franklin Delano Roosevelt to his first term has *hope* figured so prominently in the national mood. Barack Obama embodied the hopes of the disenfranchised and the disconsolate who were buoyed by his electoral victory. A year after his election, that buoyancy was replaced by a certain degree of disappointment and even bitter parody. Were we hoping for the wrong things? Were we hoping for too much? Is hope indeed a thing with feathers, delicate and flighty and easily scattered by harsh realities? Or is it—as I prefer to believe—exactly what it seems to have been for human beings since time immemorial. Hope is the means by which we can endure the otherwise unendurable and to find—even in our weakest moments—a gust of wind under tired wings.

CHAPTER 19

Love

Francesco Hayez, *"The Last Farewell of Romeo and Juliet"*,
Alfredo Dagli Orti/The Art Archive at Art Resource, NY

I am the lover's eyes, and the spirit's
Wine, and the heart's nourishment.
I am a rose. My heart opens at dawn and
The virgin kisses me and places me
Upon her breast.

I am the house of true fortune, and the
Origin of pleasure, and the beginning
Of peace and tranquility. I am the gentle smile upon the
lips of beauty …

I am the poet's elation,
And the artist's revelation,
And the musician's inspiration ...

Gifts alone do not entice me;
Parting does not discourage me;
Poverty does not chase me;
Jealousy does not prove my awareness;
Madness does not evidence my presence.

—Khalil Gibran, from *Song of Love*[1]

Love is a primal emotion, a primal need, "our house of true fortune." The love of another or of an idea or of a sight or sound or cause animates our lives and can remake the world. Love wounds, and it heals. It builds and destroys. The love of a king for an Ann Boleyn changes the course of history. The love of a young man for war and glory sets in stone the foundation for civilizations from Macedonia to India. Love engenders love ... and also hate, resentment, and revenge. Love is everywhere that man abides, for better or worse. Lucretius and Cicero regarded love as an illness requiring a cure, a passion that inevitably ends badly in betrayal, loss, self-indulgence, or any number of destructive behaviors. They are hardly alone. Cultures clearly mistrust love more than they treasure it. Laws written and unwritten seek to control love through statutes relating to intimacy, marriage and adultery, divorce, child custody, and visitation rights—all in recognition of the highly combustible mix of human beings and love. It is impossible to imagine literature, art, music, poetry, or dance without the theme of love, but it is also difficult to imagine science without the love of discovery or politics without the love of power or corruption without the love of treasure.

Nearly every aspect of the human drama is expressed in the literature of love. As Mortimer Adler observes in his monumental work *The Great Ideas*, "The love between man and woman makes all the great poems contemporaneous with each other and with ourselves."[2] Even just a few of the best known love stories of Western literature represent nothing less than a comprehensive exploration of the human condition itself.

> Paris and Helen in *The Iliad*, Prince Andrew and Natasha in *War and Peace*, Swann and Odette, Troilus and Criseyde, Lancelot and Guinevere, Gatsby and Daisy, Don Quixote and Dulcinea, Jason and Medea, Dante and Beatrice, Aeneas and Dido, Tristan and Isolde, Faust and Margaret, Othello and Desdemona, Samson and Delilah, Romeo and Juliet, Rhett and Scarlet, Odysseus and Penelope, Achilles and Patroclus, Antony and Cleopatra and Adam and Eve.[3]

These narratives endure not merely because they have constructed our idea of romantic love but because they affirm the broader values that give meaning to our lives. When we fall ill or grow old and the erotic fires cool, our expectation is that the bonds that held these legendary lovers, like the bonds that hold ours, are the same and will not break.

Philosophers, historians, and poets alike distinguish among various forms of love, among which are *eros*, *agape*, and *amor*. *Eros* refers to lust and physical attraction. *Agape* is the love one might have for a neighbor or a friend. And *amor* (or romantic love) is the love of greatest complication and deepest meaning. Eros and agape are on slender threads. It is amor that is entwined with devotion, duty, justice, generosity, courage, and essential goodness. It is the love from which other virtues grow and are given full expression.

The distinction between eros and amor, obvious though it may be, does not convince everyone. The cynic may point out that love is physically driven as much if not more so than emotionally driven, and the commitments required in romantic love are great and largely unrealistic. The moral and philosophical issues are laid out plainly in this exchange in Tolstoy's short story "Kreutzer Sonata."

> "Yes, but how is one to understand what is meant by 'true love'?" said the gentleman.

"Why, it's very simple," she said, but stopped to consider. "Love? Love is an exclusive preference for one above everybody else," said the lady.

"Preference for how long? A month, two days, or half an hour?" said the gray-haired man and began to laugh.

"Excuse me, we are evidently not speaking of the same thing." ...

"Yes, I know ... you are talking about what is supposed to be, but I am talking about what is. Every man experiences what you call love for every woman."

"Oh, what you say is awful! But the feeling that is called love does exist among people, and is given not for months, but for a lifetime!"

"No it does not!"

—Leo Tolstoy, *Kreutzer Sonata*[4]

Among other things, Tolstoy is saying that our *emotional* stake is in amor, not eros, which is why the abandonment of a lover in a time of trial can only be described as a betrayal and a failure of courage and why infidelity cuts so deeply. These are wounds of the spirit.

So many tales of *true love* have informed the complexity of amor, yet one in particular touches upon almost the whole of it. Orpheus was the son of a Thracian prince and Calliopi, the muse of music. Calliopi gave her son a lyre and the gift of music to rival Apollo himself. No one—not even the beasts and the trees in the fields—could resist the spell of his sublime music. Orpheus fell deeply in love with Eurydice and she with him. They married, but she was soon after bitten by a viper and died. Utterly bereft and bearing a love so strong that it would overpower death, Orpheus descended into the underworld of Hades to plead for her release. There he played his lyre and sang a song in which he begged for the return of his beloved Euridyce. He sang so sweetly that for those few moments the torment of the shades in hell ceased and the music "drew iron tears down Pluto's cheek,/and made Hell grant what love did seek."[5]

And so Pluto, the lord of the underworld, allowed Eurydice to leave with Orpheus on one condition, namely that Orpheus must not look back at her before they both reached the upper world. But just as Orpheus emerged into daylight, his eagerness to embrace his beloved overwhelmed him, and he looked back just before Eurydice stepped out of the cavern and into the sunlight. Instantly, she disappeared, swept back forever into the world of the dead. Orpheus was inconsolable and could do nothing but wander the countryside, playing his lyre as his only consolation. Rejecting the entreaties of other women, he was set upon by a group of Maenads or wood nymphs and torn limb from limb. His severed head was found by the muses and buried in a place in Thrace, where it is said nowhere else do the nightingales sing as sweetly.

The myth of Orpheus and Eurydice embodies not only the desire of eros but the constancy, courage, and fidelity of a higher form of devotion, that of romantic love. Like all of the lovers cited earlier, however, Orpheus's story is fiction. It is idealized and of use to the culture at large to dramatize what *ought* to be. But of course, we do not exist in the realm of *ought to be* but rather in the *here and now* or as Tolstoy's cynical gray-haired man put it, "I am talking about what *is*." In the case of those of us with a debilitating illness, amor—to the extent that it ever existed in our relationships—is under siege. The cynic's challenge to *true love* runs in a loop in our minds. "Preference for how long, a month, two days, a half hour?" And to that might be added, "To what effect and what remains?"

Little research has been conducted to measure the effects of illness in a spouse on the marital relationship, but those studies that have been done are not encouraging. There are precious few people like Orpheus and Penelope (the latter being the wife of Odysseus, who waited twenty years for his return while resisting innumerable suitors). While some relationships have been found to strengthen under the stress of a debilitating illness, most weaken, and many fall apart. Compounding the problem is the fact that the partner who is ill faces consequences his or her spouse does not. As marital quality declines, practical caregiving diminishes, while at the same time, the risk of the illness *as a result* of marital strain increases. Therefore, illness brings on a cascade of difficulties and deficiencies in the marital relationship that begin to fuel each other.

In a national sample of 1,298 married couples, for example, it was found that failing health "has an adverse effect on marital quality. Changes in financial circumstances, shifts in the division of household labor, declines in marital activities, and the problematic behavior of the afflicted individual account for much of the health-marital quality relationship."[6] Another study found that marital quality among relatively healthy couples correlates with changes in physical health, suggesting that deterioration in marital quality raises the risk of declining health.[7]

And yet one Orpheus comes to mind in addition to the mythological one. His name is John Bayley, the literary critic and novelist husband of the writer and philosopher Iris Murdoch.

After more than forty years of marriage, Murdoch develops Alzheimer's disease, and Bayley is her sole caregiver. He recounts the experience in *Elegy for Iris*, a book that celebrates—without a hint of mawkishness—the enduring and astonishing power of love. Bayley divides his book into two parts, "Then" and "Now." The "Then" section recounts the extraordinary life Bayley and Murdoch enjoyed together, deeply in love while preserving their own individuality and even solitude. The "Now" section is Bayley's day-to-day caring for Iris. "The power of concentration has gone, along with the ability to form coherent sentences and to remember where she is, or has been. She does not know she has written 26 remarkable novels, as well as her books on philosophy; received honorary doctorates from the major universities; become a Dame of the British Empire."[8]

In her review of *Iris* for the *New York Times*, the novelist Mary Gordon refers to Bayley's devotion as "heroic love," not a term found in the usual lexicon of love but a fitting description nonetheless.[9] And so it *is* heroic love. When a woman whose husband is also afflicted with Alzheimer's asks

Bayley rhetorically, "It's like being chained to a corpse, isn't it?" Bayley is repelled by the remark but sees no relevance to his own circumstance. "Iris is Iris," he writes.[10]

"When the body is no longer desired," observes the novelist Jeffrey Eugenides, "when beauty has faded, when possessiveness has been relinquished, real love shows its face. This seems to happen most often in old age or as the result of a winnowing of ego. Born with desire ... we grow into love, and then only sometimes, and only if we're lucky."[11]

In caring for Iris as her generous, rich, and brilliant mind dissolves and she recedes into oblivion, Bayley follows her in her descent. Unlike Orpheus, he does not plead for the release of his lover, for there is nothing to plead for that can be granted. There is only the thing to be endured. Bayley is content to simply be there for his wife, whom he still regards as "just Iris." There is nothing more complicated or more human than holding hands without speaking. It is an act of love to enter this way into another's zone of suffering "where nothing is offered or promised."[12] Sometimes that is enough.

CHAPTER 20

Despair

Edvard Munch, *"Despair"*, Erich Lessing/Art Resource, NY

[Hamlet] O, that this too too sallied flesh
would melt Thaw and resolve itself into a dew!

Or that the Everlasting had not fix'd
His canon 'gainst self-slaughter! O God! God!
How weary, stale, flat and unprofitable,
Seem to me all the uses of this world!
Fie on't! ah fie! 'tis an unweeded garden,
That grows to seed; things rank and gross in nature
Possess it merely.

—William Shakespeare, *Hamlet*[1]

It seems to be in the nature of human beings to be hopeful even when things seem bleakest. Perhaps this has to do with our powers of imagination and our instinct for creating narratives to make sense of things. In a collection of her nonfiction writing, Joan Didion declares as much in the book's title, *We Tell Ourselves Stories in Order to Live.* If we can *imagine* how something we hope for might happen, then we can see our way to the possibility that it will happen. A lover leaves. We construct the story that the man will come to regret his infidelity, realize his loss, and return. A teenage son is out much later than usual with the family car. He must have just lost track of the time and is safe at a friend's house. We're afflicted with an illness. Researchers are always working. Therefore, a cure might be discovered at any time, even soon.

In contrast to hopefulness, despair is a *failure* of the imagination. When we are in despair, no remedy can be conjured. All pathways appear closed, a plausible narrative leading to daylight cannot be found. Everywhere we look, we find only a dead end. In Hamlet's famous lament, which began this chapter, Hamlet expresses his distress over his father's death and the marriage of his mother to his uncle (his father's brother) within just a month. He considers her hasty remarriage to be an unbearable outrage. It is all too much for him. He can no longer take pleasure in anything. He sees no way out, and he is certain that all this "cannot come to good."[2]

And yet as deeply melancholic and searing as despair can be, I would argue that it is different from *depression*. Depression, including bipolar disorder and other forms of the condition, are pathologies subject to clinical diagnosis and medicinal remedy. Certainly, people who are depressed experience despair, but the inverse is not always the case. People in despair are not necessarily clinically depressed. Despair is often the result of a rational mind coming to a carefully reasoned conclusion that circumstances and objective evidence have closed off all benign outcomes. A perfectly *normal* emotional response to such a calculation is despair, which might be defined as the *considered* abandonment of hope.

In his poem "The Second Coming," written in 1920, Yeats presages the calamities yet to be visited on mankind as the century lumbers forward. Having borne witness to the slaughter and moral chaos of World War I, a pandemic that killed millions, an exhausted Europe and a society adrift in the wreckage of its own best values and institutions, Yeats sees "the second coming" as apocalyptic rather than redemptive. It is not the second coming of Christ but of something monstrous.

> Turning and turning in the widening gyre
> The falcon cannot hear the falconer;
> Things fall apart; the centre cannot hold;
> Mere anarchy is loosed upon the world,
> The blood-dimmed tide is loosed, and everywhere
> The ceremony of innocence is drowned;
> The best lack all conviction, while the worst
> Are full of passionate intensity.
>
> Surely some revelation is at hand;
> Surely the Second Coming is at hand.
> The Second Coming! Hardly are those words outWhen a
> vast image out of Spiritus Mundi
> Troubles my sight: somewhere in sands of the desert
> A shape with lion body and the head of a man,
> A gaze blank and pitiless as the sun,
> Is moving its slow thighs, while all about it
> Reel shadows of the indignant desert birds.
> The darkness drops again; but now I know
> That twenty centuries of stony sleep

> Were vexed to nightmare by a rocking cradle,
> And what rough beast, its hour come round at last,
> Slouches towards Bethlehem to be born?

—W. B. Yeats, "The Second Coming"[3]

Yeats provides us with a reasoned argument and a disturbing portent of things to come. He tells us that "the falcon cannot hear the falconer." The fortifying voice of the traditional moral order has been drowned out by the noise of new ideologies and the clamor of a world where everything is permitted. Some new "rough beast," made all the more dangerous for being half man, is becoming restive. A second coming is looming, destined to be as consequential a birth—if not as benign—as another which occurred in Bethlehem.

This beast that Yeats imagines had been in the making for nearly a century prior to his poetic vision of it. As the modern world began to take form in the nineteenth century, a burgeoning industrial and technological society awakened the unsettled resentments and political divisions of Europe. Progress exacted a great toll. Traditional values and institutions—most especially the family—began to crack under the seductions of material advancement. The stresses became too great. The center did not hold. A world war solved nothing and only served to plant the seeds of as yet unimagined catastrophe. There were new diversions, to be sure, but beneath it all was a sense of foreboding, of matters lumbering toward no good.

Yeats envisions a society that is ill and progressively so. That rough beast slouching toward Bethlehem and waiting to be born might just as well refer to literal illness as to the gathering of historic forces. Yeats hears the rumble of a grim destiny approaching, and whether it is the destiny of nations or the progressing illness of a single man or woman, the sound and the terror is the same.

Despair is emotional quicksand. For those of us afflicted with debilitating and chronic illnesses, despair carries the certitude of inescapable fate. It is all we can do to prevent despair from becoming a permanent state of mind. But that is what we *have to do*; otherwise despair becomes a leaden descent to oblivion. We cannot control circumstances. The rough beast will be born. But that does not have to be the end of it. There has to be something we find in ourselves "which persists through all the deadening force of circumstance."[4]

The logic of despair—as opposed to the pathology of clinical depression—has dispassionately considered the *facts* and *reality*. The conclusion is that all is lost. All remedies are deemed to be irrelevant or ineffectual. There is, however, a fatal flaw in its dark logic. It almost always fails to appreciate the role of *chance*—an unpredictable, completely surprising simple twist of fate. It is the sort of randomness, blind luck, and "bolt from the blue" that rational calculations invariably omit. Yet these occurrences more often than not determine the direction of our lives. The writing of this very chapter is a case in point.

After making the point regarding the often decisive role of chance, I intended to discuss Thomas Hardy's novel *Jude the Obscure*[5] as an example of a book of utterly complete and unrelieved despair. But in an extraordinary coincidence, the very sort of unexpected event that is unaccounted for by those in despair *actually occurred during the writing of the chapter*. First, let's look at a synopsis of Hardy's journey into the darker regions of human experience.

Hardy's novel expresses his deep pessimism regarding the human condition and the soul-crushing strictures of nineteenth century Victorian England. Published in 1895, *Jude the Obscure* portrays the short life of Jude Fawley, a young man with scholarly and religious ambitions whose every choice leads to catastrophe. He marries Arabella, a young woman of no merit and few scruples, and is driven to attempt suicide. He subsequently falls in love with Sue, a woman betrothed to his friend and mentor, Richard Phillotson. Eventually, Jude and Sue declare their love openly and live together only to be ostracized by their Victorian community. Soon they become itinerants with three children in tow. Bitter and despondent, Sue mentions to the eldest child, Little Father Time, that children ought not be brought into this horrible world. In his simpleton's innocence to make the world a better place, Little Father Time hangs himself and his two siblings from coat hooks. Sue finally leaves Jude and returns to Phillotson. Jude's health deteriorates, and he dies in physical and spiritual misery. In a final ironic insult to life itself, Arabella, with whom he had been reunited near the end, finds him dead in his bed but prefers to attend a picnic with her randy friends before troubling herself to summon the undertaker.

Was Jude's tortured existence entirely his doing? Perhaps, but perhaps not. Had he not chanced upon three country girls as a youth, he would never have married Arabella. Had Sue not expressed her frustration to Little Father Time in a chance moment, three children might not have died. Had Jude met Sue before Arabella or before Phillotson had, he might have married Sue legitimately and led a reasonably happy life.

Events in *Jude the Obscure* seem inevitable. One clearly disastrous choice follows another as Jude's own rough beast slouches toward its birth and Jude's ultimate demise. Jude's despair and spiritual descent is not irrational; it is reasonable. And as it turned out, his fate was sealed, and salvation from this monstrous existence was not to be.

As these lines were written for the purpose of arguing that one fewer random meeting, one fewer happenstance might have altered Jude's downward trajectory as any unpredictable happenstance might well alter ours, I received this "breaking news" e-mail from the Michael J. Fox Foundation:

March 3, 2010:

On March 1, 2010, Parkinson's researchers <u>funded in part by The Michael J. Fox Foundation</u> announced they had developed a vaccine that reverses an experimental form of Parkinson's Disease in a pre-clinical model.

The Michael J. Fox Foundation spoke to Scientific Advisory Board member <u>David : Standaert, MD, PhD,</u> of the University of Alabama at Birmingham about the research, next steps and possible implications for patients.

<u>Read our in-depth interview with Dr. Standaert,</u> now posted on the Foundation's Web site, o gain a clearer understanding of the news and what it may mean for people with PD." [6]

—MJFF, "Breaking News" general announcement,
March 3, 2010

A seemingly random and unforeseen event (though not random to the researchers at the University of Alabama) suddenly breaks the certitude of despair. No one knows whether this flicker of light will illuminate a path to the curing Parkinson's disease. Nonetheless, the stone wall of despair sustained a crack. For all his obvious faults and self-delusion, Jude Fawley might in the end have been more sinned against than sinning, and as one critic noted, "a luckless man."[7] But as any gambler will confirm, there is always the possibility of a turn of luck.

CHAPTER 21

Friendship

Sosius Painter, *"Achilles Binding Patroclus's Wounds"*, Red Figure drinking
cup, from Vulci, c. 500 BCE.bpk, Berlin/Art Resource, NY

Let me not to the marriage of true minds
Admit impediments. Love is not love
Which alters when it alteration finds,
Or bends with the remover to remove:
O no! it is an ever-fixed mark
That looks on tempests and is never shaken;
It is the star to every wandering bark,
Whose worth's unknown, although his height
be taken.

Love's not Time"'s fool, though rosy lips and
cheeks
Within his bending sickle's compass come:
Love alters not with his brief hours and weeks,
But bears it out even to the edge of doom.
If this be error and upon me proved,
I never writ, nor no man ever loved.

—William Shakespeare, "Sonnet 116"[1]

The claim by some people that they have dozens or even scores of "friends" has always struck me as an innocent but great exaggeration. A friend, particularly one described as *close*, implies a level of trust and affection that seems impossible to maintain with very many people at once.

Individuals will of course define *friend* differently. Some will be more discriminating than others, and many may see little distinction between a friend and say that it's an acquaintance of long standing. If high school and college buddies whom we haven't seen for decades are included—as well as that delightful couple we met on vacation last year—then one's circle of friends can become fairly expansive. This is all to the good. The illusion of numberless friends is a useful psychological and cultural device. It is comforting to think that many people care for us (and we for them), and it is helpful in knitting communities together.

In times of trial, however, especially those involving serious illness, the term *friend* carries higher expectations. Whereas in relatively carefree days, friendship is defined by compatibility or amiability or like-mindedness, but tougher times call for tougher stuff—devotion, selflessness, genuine affection, or even sacrifice.

Illness sets us apart from normalcy however much we may resist. We are drawn into a zone of our own where we contend daily with our infirmities many of which are invisible to others and often remain so by our choice. A friend is one who—perhaps by intuition but surely by a refined understanding of us—reaches into that space with a word or hand and makes things more bearable. "A friend may well be reckoned the masterpiece of nature", writes Emerson. "It is for aid and comfort through all the relations and passages of life and death. It is fit for serene days, and graceful gifts, and country rambles, but also for rough roads and hard fare, shipwreck, poverty, and persecution. We are to … embellish it by courage, wisdom, and unity."[2]

The point is that true friendship is not a social skill. It is not a show of compassion which can just as easily be directed toward perfect strangers. It is a special form of human intimacy not readily found among the battalions who in ordinary times may be classified as "friends".

Emerson and Michel de Montaigne, who are regarded as two of the greatest essayists of Western literature, both address the subject of friendship and celebrate its unique and even exclusionary nature. "Friendship," writes Emerson, "may be said to require natures so rare and costly, each so well tempered and so happily adapted … that its satisfaction can very seldom be assured. It cannot subsist in its perfection, say some of those who are learned in this warm lore of the heart, betwixt more than two."[3] Emerson is echoing Montaigne, who nearly three centuries earlier had been even more direct in asserting that there could be only one ideal friendship in our lives.

> This perfect friendship of which I speak is indivisible, each gives himself so entirely to his friend that he has nothing to dispose of elsewhere; on the contrary, he is grieved that he is not double, triple, or quadruple, and that he has not several souls and several wills, to bestow them all on that object. Ordinary friendships can be divided: one may love the beauty of this person, the courtesy of another, the liberality of another; the paternal affection of one man, the brotherly love of another, and so forth; but the friendship that possess the soul and rules over it in full sovereignty—it is impossible that it should be double.
>
> —Michel de Montaigne, "Of Friendship"[4]

Montaigne notwithstanding, we certainly have the capacity for more than one true friend, as Emerson also concedes. But the friend archetype in literature very often seems to be "betwixt two," which allows perhaps for a more sharply drawn and effective dramatization of the qualities that bind one friend to the other.

Chief among those qualities of friendship is devotion, which arises from love rather than from duty or obligation. True friendship is given freely for its own sake, not for ulterior motives. According to Montaigne, friendships "are less beautiful and noble" and far less true "[when] they introduce another cause and end and fruit into friendship than friendship itself." [5] We appreciate how true this is each time perfunctory calls asking how we're "coming along" or obligatory visits leave us with a certain sadness. There is a chill in that sort of ritual. For Montaigne, a friend becomes a true friend simply "because it was he, because I was I."[6]

There are innumerable instances in literature that reflect the intensity and honesty of friendships as imagined by Emerson and Montaigne. Among them are a small handful that seem to me to be particularly notable for their representation of what it is we ought to expect from a friend and what we ought to be willing to give.

Perhaps the earliest fully realized literary portrayal of a great friendship in the Western canon is that of Achilles and Patroclus in Homer's *The Iliad*. Achilles, the Greeks' fiercest warrior in the war against Troy, has withdrawn from the fight in a rage after being forced to surrender a favorite concubine to Agamemnon, the commander in chief of the Greeks.

There has been much conjecture regarding whether or not Achilles's love for Patroclus was erotic as well as fraternal since erotic love between otherwise heterosexual males was not unusual in ancient Greek culture. Suffice it to say that Achilles and Patroclus were deeply devoted friends, so much so that Patroclus had no compunction about rebuking the godlike Achilles, a liberty others would not dare take.

As Achilles indulges his rage and remains out of action, the Trojans led by their magnificent hero, Hector, are routing the Greeks and could soon reach and torch the beached Greek armada. Patroclus admonishes Achilles for his stubbornness and pleads with him to return to the battle. He refuses, but agrees to allow Patroclus to wear his distinctive armor as a ruse. After Patroclus leaves, Achilles prays for his safe return and pours a libation to Zeus from a golden cup reserved only for offerings to him. It is a rare tender moment in an otherwise blood-soaked epic of war and brutality.

The plan for Patroclus to impersonate Achilles has the intended effect. The Greeks are reenergized at the seeming reengagement of Achilles. The Trojans are stricken with terror, and the tide of battle turns against the Trojans. A formidable warrior himself, Patroclus hacks through the retreating Trojan lines until he comes face-to-face with Hector. Achilles had warned Patroclus not to challenge Hector under any circumstances, but Patroclus disobeys his friend and is killed. As a final humiliation, Hector strips Patroclus of Achilles's armor, and the fight now is for possession of the hero's corpse.

It is through Homer's recounting of Achilles's utter devastation on hearing the news of Patroclus's death and his subsequent pursuit of Hector to exact revenge that we are given to understand the depth and quality of his friendship with Patroclus. It is a relationship between men of war and action and therefore expressed in the context of violence and death. Fictional and remote as that relationship and its circumstances may seem to be to us, it serves as a metaphor of devotion that is profoundly human and timeless.

When Achilles is told of the death of Patroclus, his grief is unrestrained.

> A black cloud of grief came shrouding over Achilles.
> Both hands clawing the ground for soot and filth,
> He poured it over his head, fouled his handsome face
> And black ashes settled onto his fresh clean war-shirt.
> Overpowered in all his power, he sprawled in the dust.
> Achilles lay there, fallen …
> tearing his hair, defiling it with his own hands.
>
> —Homer, *The Iliad* [7]

154

The key phrase here is "overpowered in all his power." As grand and magnificent and godlike as Achilles is, the magnitude of his loss is greater. Achilles's mother, Thetis, a goddess who bore him in her marriage with a mortal king, attempts to console him. Yet he is inconsolable.

> But what joy to me now? My dear comrade's dead—
> Patroclus—the man I loved beyond all other comrades.
> Loved as my own life—I've lost him—Hector's killed him.

Homer, *The Iliad*[8]

Here Homer expresses the feeling we have that a friend is a part of us, and therefore, his death is in some way a death for us as well. Homer presages by a millennium Montaigne, who observed, "[Friends] are blended and melted one into another in a commingling so entire that they lose sight of that which first united them and cannot again find it."[9] From the depths of his grief, Achilles vows revenge and summons a bloodlust for Hector equal in intensity to his love for Patroclus.

> My spirit rebels—I've lost the will to live,
> To take my stand in the world of men—unless,
> Before all else, Hector's battered down by my spear
> And gasps away his life, the blood-price for Patroclus,
> Monoetius' gallant son he's killed and stripped!"

Homer, *The Iliad*[10]

Achilles's boundless love for Patroclus now finds expression in his matchless, irresistible ferocity. Putting aside his rage toward Agamemnon, Achilles reenters the battle and slaughters Trojans by the dozens, all the time searching for Hector. Finally, he engages him just outside the walls of Troy, and Achilles is the victor.

As Hector "crashed in the dust/godlike Achilles gloried over him:/'Hector— surely you thought when you stripped Patroclus' armor/that you, you would be safe! Never a fear of me—/... you fool! ... the great avenger waited ... [Now] the dogs and birds will maul you, shame your corpse/

while Achaeans bury my dear friend in glory!"[11] To the horror of Hector's royal parents and the people of Troy watching from the ramparts Achilles strips Hector of his captured armor, lashes his body behind his chariot, and circles the city of Troy, dragging Hector's corpse back to the Greek camp.

And so Achilles's revenge is complete. The fate of Troy is sealed, and he has come closer to meeting his own destiny. In the course of this epic, bloody narrative—in this dance of love and death among Achilles, Patroclus, and Hector—Homer illuminates the better angels of the human heart and affects us all the more by doing so against the backdrop of its demons—hate, vengeance, and brutality. On the one hand, we see an open, honest, and loving relationship, but on the other, implacable rage and walls of fighting words. Grief for a fallen friend finds its counterpoint in the mutilation of an enemy. Amid the carnage of war and the chaos of life itself, love and devotion somehow endure, contained in the intimacy of friends.

The bond between friends is so profound, Montaigne observed, that friends somehow are "commingled" and, as he described it, "melted one into another." As most of us have learned through personal experience, this often happens quietly without fanfare and evolves as a mutually felt state of mind. It is the feeling we have when we know what a friend is thinking before he or she states the thought or when we know he or she seems unsettled by some unexpressed vexation.

This intuitive sense of connectedness seems to be a primal human quality. It is everywhere evident in our everyday lives and most especially in the formative literature of our culture. In Genesis, the notion of physical as well as spiritual connection is clearly expressed in the creation of Eve from Adam's rib in order that he be "completed" and provided with a "help meet." "And Adam said, This is now 'bone of my bone', and 'flesh of my flesh' … Therefore shall a man leave his father and his mother, and shall cleave unto his wife; and they shall be one flesh."[12] Thus, friends and lovers are one and the same. In the New Testament, Christ offers up His body and blood in communion with His disciples, signifying the unity and comity of the brotherhood of man. In mythology, Castor and Pollux are friends and twins, but only Pollux is immortal. When Castor dies, Pollux asks Zeus to take from him a portion of his own immortality and give it to his friend. Zeus grants his request and transforms Castor and Pollux into the Gemini Twins constellation, which stands in silent testimony to the sanctity and power of friendship even "to the edge of doom … So sang of old love's poet."[13]

Most friendships are not nearly as heroic or dramatic as these and would not make for storylines that endure for millennia. Most of us lead ordinary lives and with some luck share it with a small handful of true friends. When illness strikes, they remain. The relationship not having rested on sand but on stone, their constancy is a comfort and a kind of cure.

CHAPTER 22

On Being Ill

Otto Dix, "*The Match Vendor*", Erich Lessing/Art Resource, NY

Illness is the nightside of life, a more onerous citizenship. Everyone who is born holds dual membership, in the kingdom of the well and in the kingdom of the sick. Although we prefer to use only the good passport, sooner or later each of us is obliged, at least for a spell. To identify ourselves as citizens of that other place.

—Susan Sontag, *Illness as Metaphor*[1]

There is something bred in the bone that is evoked in us when we receive a diagnosis of a serious illness like Parkinson's. Suddenly, we and our loved ones experience a sense of vulnerability perhaps as never before, not merely with respect to the immediate effects of disease but to all of its consequences, most especially the possibility of extended decline. The life we've known and the life we intended to live has forever been altered. The specter of loss materializes like a threatening sky, and our small tribe is shaken and fearful. A weak link has been exposed. Some friends begin to peel away as others draw near. Our illness changes everything.

In contrast, the world at large remains sublimely indifferent. We, on the other hand, have experienced an earthquake. The earth has shifted on its axis, and mountains have crumbled. Yet around us no one and nothing seems to have taken notice. The green grocer that we pass on the way home from the doctor's office places his produce carefully in its place as is his habit. Not a leaf stirs differently than it otherwise would. Car traffic flows as before. Our illness changes nothing but us.

We have been transported from the safe and familiar world of everyday rhythms to uncharted territory. We cannot help but feel apart from *normal* people who, hard as they might try, cannot fathom the magnitude of our displacement or fully appreciate as we do now the countless blessings of good health. We are distanced even from our most empathetic friends and family. Virginia Woolf bears witness to this sense of isolation in her essay, "On Being Ill" when she states, "[In illness] the whole landscape of life lies remote and fair, like the shore seen from a ship far out at sea."[2] She echoes this same sentiment later in her novel *To the Lighthouse*.

"See the little house," he said pointing, wishing Cam to look.

She raised herself reluctantly and looked. But which was it? She could no longer make out, there on the hillside, which was their house. All looked distant and peaceful and strange. The shore seemed refined, far away, unreal. Already the little distance they had sailed had pulled them far from it and given it the changed look, the composed look, of something receding in which one has no longer any part.

—Virginia Woolf, *To the Lighthouse*[3]

In our growing isolation, we feel voiceless. How do we express the fear? How do we bridge the chasm between us without seeming needy or self-indulgent? Who speaks for the afflicted? Woolf argues that literature fails to provide suitable surrogates or comfort.

Considering how common illness is, how tremendous the spiritual change that it brings, how astonishing when the lights of health go down, the undiscovered countries that are then disclosed, what wastes and deserts of the soul a slight attack of influenza brings to view, what precipices and lawns sprinkled with bright flowers a little rise of temperature reveals, what ancient and obdurate oaks are uprooted in us by the act of sickness … it becomes strange indeed that illness has not taken its place with love and battle and jealousy among the prime themes of literature. Novels, one would have thought, would have been devoted to influenza, epic poems to typhoid: odes to pneumonia; lyrics to toothache.

—Virginia Woolf, *On Being Ill*[4]

Woolf was not overstating the level of resistance to writing about illness. George Bernard Shaw declared that "disease is not interesting; it is something to be done away with by general consent, and that is all about it."[5] And even much more recently, John Updike, who himself was afflicted his whole life with psoriasis, felt very much as Shaw did, remarking that

160

illness was one area of life that could not be made interesting to the reader. "Disease and pain, for instance, are of consuming concern to the person suffering from them, but their descriptions weary us within a few paragraphs." [6]

The fact is that English and American literature of the eighteenth and nineteenth centuries did feature characters whose illness affected the narrative. For the most part, however—and this is Woolf's central point—illness tended to be romanticized rather than honestly explored. Being ill might have acted as a force for creativity in the artist, but it was rarely the subject of lyrical expression within the work itself. Tuberculosis, for example, or "consumption," as it was called, was quite common during this period. It had a certain glamour about it and was not viewed as entirely tragic. "I should like to die of a consumption," Lord Byron once said, "because the ladies would all say, 'look at that poor Byron, how interesting he looks in dying.'"[7] And of Frederic Chopin, it was written, "Chopin was tubercular [1848] at a time when good health was not chic. It was fashionable to be pale and drained; Princess Beligijoso strolled along the boulevards pale as death in person."[8]

Woolf published "On Being Ill" in 1926. However, as the twentieth century rumbled on, illness became a more common literary subject as Woolf had hoped. Perhaps it was a consequence of a century in which human mortality was experienced on an unprecedented, horrific scale—a worldwide pandemic, two world wars, countless revolutions, and civil wars resulted in the death of many, many millions—all against the paradoxical backdrop of dramatic advances in medical science. Illness and violent death ravaged the world in the twentieth century.

A fair compilation of the works that have made the greatest contribution to writing about illness would almost certainly include John Gunther's *Death Be Not Proud* (1949), Elizabeth Kubler-Ross's On *Death and Dying* (1972), Susan Sontag's *Illness as Metaphor* (1978), which will be addressed later in this chapter, and Anatole Broyard's *Intoxicated by My Illness* (1992). Broyard speaks directly of the liberating effect a serious illness has on personal expression. "A critical illness is like a great permission, an authorization or absolving. It's all right for a threatened man to be romantic, even crazy, if he feels like it. All your life you think you have to hold back your craziness, but when you're sick you can let it go in all its garish colors."⁹

In her seminal book *Illness as Metaphor*, Susan Sontag—unlike Woolf—is not concerned with describing what it is like to be ill but rather with illuminating how the experience of illness is affected by language and culture. Sontag argues that the metaphors surrounding specific diseases (her main focus is on tuberculosis and cancer) deeply prejudice our encounter with these illnesses and how others view those who are afflicted. "It is hardly possible, " she writes, "to take up residence in the kingdom of the ill unprejudiced by the lurid metaphors with which it has been landscaped."[11]

The metaphors that apply to illness in general and to particular diseases are the means by which a culture explains illness to itself. In doing so, it oversteps and often defies medical science. If the presumption is that health represents the body in *good order*, then disease is the body in *disorder*, which may be the result of social and spiritual forces as well as physical phenomena. An extreme and repugnant example is the view among some people that AIDS is God's punishment for a dissolute lifestyle. But we do not need to go so far afield. Sontag reminds us,

> As once TB was thought to come from too much passion, afflicting the reckless and sensual, today many people believe that cancer is a disease of insufficient passion, afflicting those who are sexually repressed, inhibited, unspontaneous, incapable of expressing anger … For both psychological accounts of a disease stress the insufficiency or balking of vital energies.
>
> —Susan Sontag, *Illness as Metaphor*[12]

The notion that illness is a state of disorder—or more accurately, of imperfection—is at the root of our contemporary conviction that all diseases can be cured. It is just a matter of finding the physiological or genetic or environmental causes and remediating them. This may well be true, and everyone hopes that it is. However, in opposition to the conceptual framework of *abnormality* or *deficiency* or *disorder* or *genetic damage* is the counterintuitive idea that disease is in fact a normal part of the process of life. Yet nowhere in the modern lexicon of disease and its treatment are we presented with the bias that says, "Your illness simply *is*. It has no proximate cause other than life itself, but with medical science, it may be possible to overcome it or eliminate or delimit its effects." Our metaphors do not allow for such equanimity.

How can words affect our experience of so profound a reality as being ill? Sontag is careful to point out that there's nothing abstract about being sick. The reality of being debilitated or in pain or driven to distraction and depression by fear cannot be overstated. However, the fact is that the *burden* of illness can be made heavier or lighter by words. Nowhere is this more clearly expressed than in Aldous Huxley's *Words and Their Meanings*.

> A great deal of attention has been paid ... to the technical languages in which men of science do their specialized thinking ... But the colloquial usages of everyday speech ... have been strangely neglected. We talk about "mere matters of words" in a tone which implies that we regard words as things beneath the notice of a serious-minded person.
>
> This is a most unfortunate attitude. For the fact is that words play an enormous part in our lives and are therefore deserving of the closest study. The old idea that words possess magical powers is false; but its falsity is the distortion of a very important truth. Words do have a magical effect—but not in the way that magicians supposed, and not on the objects they were trying to influence. Words are magical in the way they affect the minds of those who use them. "A mere matter of words," we say contemptuously, forgetting that words have the power to mould men's thinking, to canalize their feeling, to direct their willing and acting. Conduct and character

are largely determined by the nature of the words we currently use to discuss ourselves and the world around us.

—Aldous Huxley, *Words and Their Meanings*[13]

In 1817, the English surgeon James Parkinson gave his name to the neurological disorder that had for at least two hundred years been referred to in modern English as "the shaking palsie" and before that simply as "tremor." According to the *Oxford English Dictionary*, "shaking palsie" first appeared in the literary record in 1615, specifically in Crooke's *Body of Man*. Shaking along with its connotations has remained the dominant metaphor of the illness, and it has attach itself to the reference "Parkinson's disease." Shaking brings to mind frailty, fear, ineffectualness, vulnerability, unsteadiness, advancing age, helplessness—words that cannot help but manifest themselves in the self-image of those afflicted and in the minds of those who interact with them.

Words and metaphors count as Sontag so persuasively argues. However, while they may be long-lived, they are not immutable. In recent years embedded ideas of what it means to be ill with Parkinson's have been challenged. What are we to make of the fact that the world's finest athlete, a champion in a sport requiring nearly superhuman quickness and steadiness in the face of physical attack, develops Parkinson's disease? Traditional metaphors are necessarily weakened, and the actuality of the disease comes into sharper focus.

Similarly, what are we to make of the fact that an illness associated with the elderly afflicts a young actor whose very fame is based on the youthful brashness of the characters he portrays? Far from being rendered ineffectual by "the shaking palsie," he launches the most significant effort to date in support of research for its cure.

I don't believe that people living with Parkinson's disease see themselves as battling the language and imagery that define it and shape their response to it. However, a twist of fate that we share has altered what we and others see and how we feel about ourselves when we are ill with Parkinson's disease.

CHAPTER 23

Where Shall Wisdom be Found?

**Lisyppos, "*Socrates*", copy of 4th c. bust.
Erch Lessing/Art Resource, NY**

But where shall wisdom be found? And where
is the place of understanding?

165

Man knoweth not the price thereof; neither is
it found in the land of the living.
The depth saith, it is not in me: and the sea saith, It is not with me.
It cannot be gotten for gold, and neither shall
silver be weighed for the price thereof.
It cannot be valued with the gold of Ophir, with
the precious onyx, or the sapphire.
The gold and the crystal cannot equal it: and the
exchange of it shall not be for jewels or fine gold.
No mention shall be made of coral, or of pearls:
for the price of wisdom is above rubies,
The topaz of Ethiopia shall not equal it, neither
shall it be valued with pure gold.
Whence cometh wisdom? And where is the place of understanding?
Seeing it is hid from the eyes of all living, and
kept close from the fowls of the air.
Destruction and death say, We have heard
the fame thereof with our ears.
God understandeth the way thereof, and he knoweth the place thereof.
For he looketh to the ends of the earth, and
seeth under the whole heaven;
To make the weight for the winds; and he
weigheth the waters by measure.
When he made a decree for the rain, and a way
for the lightning of the thunder;
Then he did see it, and declare it; he prepared it, yea, and searched it out.
And unto man he said, Behold, the fear of the Lord, that
is wisdom; and to depart from evil is understanding.

—The Holy Bible, the book of Job[1]

Wisdom seems distinctly out of fashion these days. *Information* is what we're after in the twenty-first century, and apparently, the more of it, the better. Marketable skills and scientific and technological data that can be applied to commerce have become the focal points of our educational and business institutions. The word wisdom itself has taken on an ephemeral and archaic cast, bringing to mind images of ancient sages or of philosophers and theologians at a great remove from the hurly-burly of *real* life.

But it was not too long ago—perhaps even as recently as the midpoint of the twentieth century—that higher education still held to its traditional role of introducing its young charges to something approximating wisdom. Curricula emphasized the humanities (i.e., liberal arts) and exposed students to the best of what had been written and achieved in human history and encouraged them to conduct a "great conversation" with the eminences of the past.[2] The intention was to enlarge students' capacity for understanding the human condition, especially themselves and the meaning of the life they wanted to pursue. Alexander Pope's admonition that "the proper study of mankind is man"[3] and the ideals of the Enlightenment were the lodestar of American universities.

By the late twentieth century, however, that star had faded. In 2007, Anthony T. Kronman, Sterling professor of law at Yale, pronounced the humanities all but dead in his landmark book *Education's End: Why our Colleges and Universities Have Given Up on the Meaning of Life.*

> Earlier ages knew more about humanity than we do. By comparison to their steady attention to the human condition, and the great works this produced, our attention is fitful and anemic at best. We have not gained ground in our understanding of humanity as we have in our knowledge of the physical world. We have lost ground instead.
>
> —Anthony T. Kronman, *Education's End*[4]

Why has this happened? According to Professor Kronman, the rise of science and technology and their growing authority have eclipsed the humanities largely because the hard sciences offer us greater control over our world (particularly our deficiencies and infirmities).

> The science on which technology depends has the authority it does because it gratifies at once our desire

for control and our desire to understand for the sake of understanding itself. But this knowledge is not only incomplete ... It is also the cause of an important kind of ignorance precisely because is satisfies so fully our desire to be in ever control of our circumstances. Science supports the technological imperative and encourages the devaluation of morality this implies. But in doing so it promotes the forgetfulness of humanity that technology invites. Hence just because it satisfies as powerfully as it does our archaic desire for control, science frustrates the equally deep desire for understanding, so far as the understanding of ourselves is concerned.

—Anthony T. Kronman, *Education's End*[5]

To Professor Kronman's observation, I would add another. Achieving even a small measure of wisdom requires the willingness and capacity to reflect, to *contemplate*. And this in turn demands time. Yet the breakneck speed at which our lives are run makes this a challenge nearly impossible to meet. The ubiquitous electronic media bombard us with information—much of it overwhelming in quantity and indiscriminate in quality. We are perennially *connected* through *smart* phones, iPods, computers, radios, and televisions. Entertainment has reached the level of a societal addiction. Its varieties and accessibility have never been greater in the history of man or its presence more enveloping.

The irony that escapes most of us is that we're so busy being connected to others and to our amusements that we hardly notice that the price we pay is to be disconnected from ourselves. And most of this *input* to which we give much of our waking hours arrives from *favorites* and *friends*. So we engage primarily with what makes us comfortable and prescreen that which does not—hardly the road to enlightenment. As a result, many of us—particularly those born into this electronic age—live in a perfectly customized echo chamber of a thousand favorite songs and familiar voices. Consider this in light of the definition of wisdom offered by Plotinus—one of those ancients for whom wisdom was a high virtue.

> Wisdom is a condition in a being that possesses repose. Think what happens when one has accomplished the reasoning process; as soon as we have discovered the right course, we cease to reason. We rest because we have come to reason.

—Plotinus, (as cited in) *The Great Ideas of Western Thought*[6]

For Plotinus, ignorance is an agitated, chaotic state that precludes understanding. Wisdom, on the other hand, achieves a calming equilibrium, a level of insight into ourselves and the world that brings peace to body and mind. Wisdom is a release from the tyranny of disharmony and confusion. But to attain it, we need at the very least to be able to hear ourselves *think*.

And yet given the apparent indifference to the pursuit of what has traditionally been regarded as wisdom and the difficulty of actually achieving it, it would be understandable for us not just to ask, "Where shall wisdom be found?" but also to wonder, "Why look?" As Harold Bloom, America's preeminent literary scholar, has observed, "Most of us know that wisdom immediately goes out the door when we are in crisis."[7] Bearing Bloom's remarks in mind and considering that living with Parkinson's disease is for many of us a permanent crisis, of what use is wisdom?

Ours is an especially difficult circumstance. Not only are we subject to the normal distractions of a world designed to amuse us into a state resembling catatonia, but we also must contend with the very real intrusions and physical limitations of disease. Wisdom, after all, is elusive and certainly not curative. Some would argue—not without justification—that people living with Parkinson's need medicine, not philosophy. Others—I among them—would argue that philosophy *is* a kind of medicine.

Thus, Bloom is only partly right. Wisdom often does "go out the door" in a time of crisis, but to extend his metaphor, it does not stay outside for very long.

Those who extol the virtues of wisdom do not concede that it is impractical. On the contrary, while wisdom is often achieved through reflection and contemplation, it is not passive. It is a quality that uses knowledge to inform action. Plato, who considered wisdom one of the four great virtues in addition to temperance, courage, and justice, ascribes to it the function of directing everyday conduct.[8] When we have intractable problems, some of us seek guidance from those we deem wiser than us, and we ask them what we should *do*. The practicality of wisdom is the reason that in times of trial, physicians seek out their mentors for advice, emperors call for their viziers, and presidents for their advisers.

In 1945, as World War II came to a close and it became clear to the new president, Harry Truman, that Stalin's Soviet Union had shifted from ally to dangerous adversary, Truman turned to six "wise men." They were the intellectual elite of America's aristocracy—John McCloy, Charles Bohlen, Dean Acheson, Robert Lovett, Averell Harriman, and George Kennan.[9] Together, they devised the policy of containment, which guided American foreign policy for fifty years, shaped the modern world, and eventually succeeded in establishing the conditions that led to the disintegration of the USSR and communism itself.

What qualities did these men have that merited a book about them titled *The Wise Men*? Are there principles of wisdom?

While there are innumerable traditions that each have their own vision of what constitutes wisdom, there are common threads across time and cultures. Seemingly from the very beginning mankind has attempted to understand his circumstances whether they relate to illness or misfortune or to the beneficences that we also receive in life. "Wisdom literature" is a term applied to many texts—the Old and New Testaments and the Qu'ran included—whose purpose is to embody the accumulated wisdom of a culture or enshrine the precepts of a faith. Wisdom literature appeared as early as 2450 BC in Sumerian cuneiform tablets and in the third millennium BC in Egypt.[10]

Of course, the differences among the wisdom literature of cultures can be substantial. Judeo-Christian tradition, for example, as expressed in the two books of the Holy Bible, counsels us to adhere to unchangeable laws of God. Confucianism, on the other hand, is rooted in a sensitive and flexible discernment of changing circumstances. Wisdom (zhi) is not dogma but the ability to adjust to and accommodate life as it happens.[11] Yet despite their differences and separation in time and space, cultures seem to share important fundamental qualities of wisdom. Particular recurrent and overarching themes emerge. *Wisdom is attainable. It is achieved only through personal struggle and discovery. It is invariably good, and once attained, it fosters humility and appreciation for human limitations rather than serving as a means to power.*

The idea that a unique and elevated quality of enlightenment or wisdom exists and can be attained seems intuitive. Whether it is possessed by a shaman or sage or embodied in ritual or holy book, wisdom holds chaos at bay and makes healing possible. The path may differ, but the belief is firm. Our vision need not always be occluded. We need not always be at the mercy of ignorance or chance. In his anguish at witnessing the spiritual dissolution of his people, Jeremiah asks, "Is there no balm in Gilead? Is there no physician there?"[12] Through the generations, mankind has preferred to believe even in its darkest hours that there is a balm in Gilead. We have never tired of seeking it.

Can wisdom be learned from others, or must it arise from within each of us?

Obviously, some truths can be learned, of course, but neither in the Western nor Eastern literary canon is a unique sagacity depicted as a quality that can be taught. One must come to it oneself. In the Eastern spiritual traditions of Buddhism and Hinduism, there are masters and pupils; however, pupils must develop independently, and little is imparted from the master in the way of answers. In Herman Hesse's novel *Siddhartha,* perhaps the book most influential in introducing Eastern religion and mysticism to the West, Siddhartha discovers that the road to wisdom is solitary.

171

On the way, Siddhartha remembered all that he had experienced in the garden of Jetavanda, the teachings he had heard there from the holy Buddha, the parting from Govinda and the conversation with the illustrious One, and he was astonished that he had said things which he did not then really know. What he had said to the Buddha—that the Buddha's wisdom was inexpressible and incommunicable—and which he had experienced in an hour of enlightenment, was just what he had now set off to experience, what he was now beginning to experience. He must gain experience himself.

—Herman Hesse, *Siddhartha*[13]

There is recognition, too, that wisdom—unlike other qualities of knowing such as skill at building or cleverness in leading or mastery of words—is *always* a force for good. Other forms of knowledge can be used for evil or can be squandered. Studies have found that in the United States and other countries for which such records have been kept, IQ has increased on average nine points per generation for at least the last seventy-give years.[14] Has this paid dividends in terms of our relationships with each other or in our approach to coping with the challenges of life? Wisdom, on the other hand, is by definition tied to the attainment of good. To act wisely is to act morally and ethically and therefore to act well. The forbidden fruit in the garden of Eden was of the Tree of *Knowledge*, not the Tree of *Wisdom*. Tasting the fruit from the Tree of Knowledge led to *both* good and evil as knowledge always does. Wisdom, on the other hand, would surely have led Adam and Eve toward even greater reverence for their benevolent Creator. The creation narrative in that case would have had to change. Could we imagine that God would punish man for gaining wisdom as opposed to gaining the knowledge of evil? The redactor of Genesis (traditionally regarded as Moses) brilliant writer that he was, no doubt appreciated the distinction. The achievement of wisdom would not do as an eternally indictable offense.

It is a consistent theme, too, in the historical and literary record that wisdom must be sought or earned. It is at the center of *the quest*, perhaps the most universal of all human narratives. Plato created the academy for the purpose of seeking wisdom. Christ wandered forty days in the desert to come to terms with what lay ahead, and Moses sought the word of God at the summit of Mt. Sinai. Jason's search for the golden fleece, Don Quixote's defense of the noble and the good, the quest for the holy grail in Arthurian legend, the epic of Beowulf and Spencer's *Canterbury Tales*, all are animated by the theme of seeking wisdom or a higher state of knowledge and understanding. We are by nature questors, and without the quest, there can be no epiphany.

The quest narrative is virtually universal. The following passage is from the *Bhagavad-Gita*, among the holiest scriptures of Hinduism and one of the world's most revered and treasured texts. Here, Krishna, the manifestation of the Supreme Deity according to the Hindu faith, simply and beautifully articulates the means to a good life. The passage begins and ends with the imperatives of *the quest* for wisdom and the need to follow a path in the search for its attainment.

> Krishna [in response to the query of Prince Arjuna regarding the Right Path]:
>
> Fearlessness, singleness of soul, the will
> Always to strive for wisdom; opened hand
> And governed appetites; piety
> And love of lonely study; humbleness,
> Uprightness, heed to injure nought which lives,
> Truthfulness, slowness unto wrath, a mind
> That letteth go what others prize;
> And equanimity, and charity
> Which spieth no man's faults; and tenderness
> Towards all that suffer; a contented heart,
> Fluttered by no desires; a bearing mild,
> Modest, and grave, with manhood nobly mixed
> With patience, fortitude and purity;

An unrevengeful spirit, never given
To rate itself too high;—such be the signs,
O Indian Prince! Of him whose feet are set
On that fair path which leads to heavenly birth!

—The Baghavad-Gita[15]

The *Baghavad-Gita* not only affirms the theme of the quest. It also illuminates perhaps the most consequential and ubiquitous qualities that recur throughout the world's wisdom literature: the profound appreciation for humility and restraint. Wisdom brings the realization that mankind knows little, controls little, and is at the mercy of forces beyond his full comprehension to which he must submit.

The book of Job (in the particular verses that opened this chapter) makes clear that there are both natural and divine limits to human understanding. Upon asking, "Where shall wisdom be found? And where is the place of understanding?" scripture goes on to provide an answer, "Man knoweth not the price thereof; neither is it found in the land of the living." Wisdom, claims the Judeo-Christian tradition, is "fear of the Lord, and to depart from evil is understanding." The case is made even more strongly by the medieval Jewish sage, Jesus Ben Sira.

What is too wonderful for thee do not search,
And what is hidden from thee do not seek.
Observe only what is permitted thee,
And have no concern for mysteries.

—Jesus Ben Sira[16]

Even in traditions such as Hinduism that place no constraints on our search and encourage the attainment of transcendent wisdom, the result is Nirvana or self-abnegation. Nirvana is not *heaven* as many in the West have assumed. Rather it represents the complete dissolution of one's ego and the achievement of unity with all existence. In virtually all traditions, a state of enlightenment and holiness requires some variant of submission.

Wisdom does not lead to triumphalism but to humility, and it is at its root an act of acceptance.

The effort to cope with Parkinson's disease or any serious chronic illness is not only a struggle with physical realities but a struggle for understanding. It is no less a search for meaning than that of the archetypal heroes of our cultural narratives. We find ourselves in a life that has suddenly changed. A crisis has come, as Bloom observed, that causes much of what we thought we knew to "go out the door."

But for most of us, the things that have suddenly fled from us don't all stay away. We recognize that there *is* a wise way or a foolish way to manage this circumstance, and we gather ourselves around this conviction, sometimes successfully and sometimes not. We may place our faith in God or in reason alone, but in either case, we are after what the great sages were after—the resistance to chaos, which is what disease represents, and the reassertion of equilibrium and spiritual repose. Will this be achieved by knowing everything? By understanding everything?

As we've seen, the wise do not regard information as wisdom or information as necessarily a good thing. It is a bias of our age—perhaps even a curse—that we have internalized the notion that more information we have, the better off we are. The Internet is a window onto limitless facts. Perhaps there is even a feeling among us that we are somehow obliged to learn all we can about our affliction and would be remiss if we did not. Yet Ben Shira admonishes us, "What is hidden from thee do not seek … And have no concern for mysteries."[17] As Genesis, too, so dramatically confirms with the expulsion of Adam and Eve from Eden, there is heresy in information.

Thus, despite our relentlessly information-rich culture, the question presents itself, "Is there wisdom in choosing to forego information? Is it sometimes wiser not to know?" For example, is it wise or foolish for one newly diagnosed with ALS to hasten to learn the precise nature and likely timing of one's inevitable decline? Is it wise or foolish to know our genetic map, which might identify susceptibility to diseases for which treatments do not exist? Or is it wiser to accept the illness as it comes, if it comes, and

175

decline to seek that which is hidden from us and opt instead to humbly focus on "[those] gifts the gods may give?"

Shakespeare is the wisest of our writers in English or in any language for that matter, and Hamlet may well be the wisest fictional character ever created. In contrast to the dithering, melancholic young man he may at first appear to be, Hamlet is a brilliant observer of life and human behavior and the possessor of a matchless wit. His dilemma begins as the result of unwelcome information, not unlike a frightening diagnosis. His father, the king of Denmark, has been murdered, and the drama unfolds as he agonizes in his search for the right thing to do.

In a literal sense, Hamlet becomes ill when he learns from his father's ghost that his father was murdered by his brother, Claudius, who then seized his throne and married his widow, Hamlet's mother. Hamlet's world has spun off its axis. The only way to put things to right is to avenge his father's murder as the ghost demands. Yet Hamlet's initial response resembles very closely what today would be considered clinical depression.

His despair and confusion are such that he contemplates suicide.

> [Hamlet]: ... who would fardels bear,
> To grunt and sweat under a weary life,
> But that the dread of something after death,
> The undiscovr'd country, from whose bourn
> No traveler returns, puzzles the will
> And makes us bear those ills we have,
> Than fly to others we know not of?
> Thus conscience doth make cowards of us all.[18]

His moods are dark.

> [Claudius]: ...There's something in his soul
> O'er which his melancholy sits on brood.[19]

He sees no purpose to life.

[Hamlet]: How weary, stale, flat, and unprofitable
Seem to me all the uses of this world!
Fie on't! O fie! 'tis an unweeded garden,
That grows to seed; things rank and gross in nature
Possess it merely.[20]

Hamlet is obsessed with what he views as his mother's infidelity and haunted by the thought of her sexual union with his father's assassin. He flies into an uncontrollable rage at his mother's shamelessly quick remarriage to his father's brother and is repelled by her [perhaps] unknowing complicity in moral corruption.

[Hamlet to Gertrude]: ...Confess yourself to heaven,
Repent what's past, avoid what is to come,
And do not spread the compost on the weeds
To make them ranker ...
[Gertrude]: O Hamlet, thou hast cleft my heart in twain.[21]

He shuns his lover, Ophelia, with callous indifference and verbal abuse.

[Hamlet]: I did love you once ... You should not have believed me, for virtue can so inoculate our old stock but we shall relish of it. I lov'd you not ...
Get thee [to] a nunnr'ry, why wouldst thou be a breeder of sinners?
Go thy ways to a nunnr'y. Where's thy father?[22]

He experiences periods of self-loathing.

[Hamlet]: O what a rogue and peasant slave am I ...
for it cannot be but that I am pigeon-livered, and lack gall to make oppression bitter.[23]

And he acts impetuously when he mistakenly kills a meddling Polonius and is without remorse.

> [Hamlet]: How now? A rat? Dead for a ducat, dead. [Kills
> Polonius through the arras]
> … A bloody deed! Almost as bad, good mother, as kill a
> king and marry with his brother.[24]

The totality of Shakespeare's work presents us with such varied, deep, and inimitably expressive insights into life and the human soul that it is not an exaggeration to credit him, as one critic does, with the "invention" of the human.[25] In a way that no author before or since could equal (save Homer or the redactors of the Bible), Shakespeare introduced us to ourselves and the emotional and psychological complexities that make us *individual* human beings. Yet astonishingly, that was not his objective. He was neither moralist or revolutionary or sage. He did not view struggle as redemptive but as necessary to the maintenance of an orderly universe. He was simply a playwright. He worked hard to entertain Elizabethan audiences for which purpose he freely appropriated existing storylines and histories and held up a mirror reflecting their own moral and social order. In truth, Shakespeare invented nothing but illuminated everything.

Hamlet's journey passes through stages from shock to indecision to resolve and finally to acceptance and action. It is an odyssey familiar to many of us in crisis. As the play approaches its climax, Hamlet returns from a voyage to England arranged by King Claudius—a voyage that was supposed to have resulted in Hamlet's death were it not for his cleverness in devising an escape.

Hamlet is accompanied by his best friend, Horatio. After a period of emotional turmoil that intensified after his encounters with his father's ghost and its demands for revenge, we find Hamlet a changed man in act 5. One critic observes, "There is a new quietude in Hamlet in Act V. He no longer frets about his dead father. He no longer seems to want to make any resolution whatsoever to do anything about Claudius. He seems to adopt a kind of wise passivity, a deep kind of quietism, which really is a disinterestedness or resignation."[26]

Here, there is the unmistakable echo of Plotinus (cited earlier): "[Wisdom is] a condition in a being that possesses repose ... as soon as we have discovered the right course, we cease to reason. We rest because we have come to reason." Hamlet has become wiser. He now knows how events must unfold. There will be no happy ending. There will only be the restoration of order to a kingdom that has been rent by fratricide and a final peace for Hamlet himself. The truth he has found is that of annihilation,[27] and he will no longer shrink from it.

As Hamlet and Horatio are returning, they pass through a graveyard where a gravedigger is preparing for the burial of Ophelia, a suicide. Seeing bones strewn about, Hamlet marvels at the overarching irony of life that all of us—politicians, knaves, kings, and asses—all come to dust. We are equal and anonymous in death, and all our fretting over issues large and small, all of our pretensions are in the end meaningless. The gravedigger, who is the only character in the play capable of matching wits with Hamlet, sings as he digs and engages Hamlet in a duel of wits. At one point, the gravedigger unearths a skull, and what follows is one of the most famous passages in literature and among the wisest and stark reflections on mortality as may be found anywhere. The skull belonged to Yorick, the king's jester and Hamlet's surrogate father and playmate. Hamlet picks it up.

> [Hamlet]: Alas, poor Yorick! I knew him, Horatio, a fellow of infinite jest, of most excellent fancy. He hath bore me on his back a thousand times, and now how abhorr'd in my imagination it is! my gorge rises at it. Here hung those lips I have kiss'd I know not how oft. Where be your gibes now, your gambols, your songs, your flashes of merriment, that were wont to see the table on a roar? Not one now to mock your own grinning—quite chop fall'n ... Prithee, Horatio, tell me one thing.
>
> [Horatio]: What's that my lord?
>
> [Hamlet]: Dost thou think Alexander looked a' this fashion I' th earth?

[Horatio]: E'en so.

[Hamlet]: To what base uses we may return, Horatio! Why may not imagination trace the noble dust of Alexander, till a' find it stopping a bunghole?

[Horatio]: 'T were to consider too curiously to consider so.

[Hamlet]: No, faith, not a jot, but to follow him thither with modesty enough and likelihood to lead it: Alexander dies: Alexander was buried, Alexander returneth to dust, the dust is earth, of earth we make loam, and why of that loam whereto he was converted might they not stop a beer barrel?

[Hamlet]: Imperious Caesar, dead and turned to clay,

Might stop a hole to keep the wind away.[28]

In the end, there is a spate of deaths, most notably that of Hamlet himself, who is killed in a duel with Ophelia's brother, Laertes, but not before he slays Claudius, his father's murderer. The throne passes, as it should, to a conquering hero, young Fortinbras of Norway. The guilty have been punished, but so too have the innocent. It is the way of the world and the lot of mankind that justice and order must exist side by side with injustice and chaos.

The struggle between these poles is nothing less than the struggle between good and evil, meaning and meaninglessness, truth and untruth. This drama occurs for each of us in that span of time that contains our lives and that may well be but "a sleep and a forgetting."[29] It may be destined—as Hamlet believes—only to come to dust. But it is the time that we have and the effort to live it with a measure of wisdom, imperfect and incomplete as it must be, that is illuminating and ennobling. This is the refrain we hear resonating through the ages if we are of a mind to listen.

CHAPTER 24

Words

Pohto by G. Nimatallah, "Gates of Auschwitz Concentration Camp", DeA Picture Library/Art Resource, NY

But I say unto you, That every idle word that men shall speak, they shall give account thereof in the day of judgment.

For by thy words thou shalt be justified, and by thy words thou shalt be condemned.

—The Holy Bible, Matthew[1]

Most of us take words for granted. They're just there for our use like the air we breathe. And our impression tends to be that communicating with one another is a matter of finding the right words to express the thoughts we've already formulated in our minds. We recognize that some people are much better at this process than others—great orators or writers or poets. The rest of us make do with a language ability that is innate and (we think) more or less suited to our needs despite occasional fumbling.

The problem with this model—that language is "out there" to be cherry-picked in order to express "what's in here"—is misleading. It gives the impression that we're in *command* of language. That's far from being the case.

Language and words are external public inventions. They're communal property. They mean what the consensus says they mean. Yet our thoughts and feelings are internal experiences and wholly unique to each of us. Therefore, despite the illusion that words express what is in our heads, they never align perfectly with what we think or feel. Words are always approximations.

The best we can hope for is that the words we choose succeed in conveying a semblance of our felt experience. This takes work. A wonderful passage by the great Texas writer and educator J. Frank Dobie makes the point that with care and facility, we can certainly be more precise in our use of language. But he also makes a less obvious but much more important observation. Words *compel* us to see and think in ways that would not be possible without them.

> A speaker poverty-stricken in vocabulary ... has but one word to express locomotion, let us say, the word "go". Hence for him all people go to the market, go to the banquet, go to the river to swim; for the moving of "every living thing of all flesh" he has but one word, "go". Were it given to him to behold a second hegira of all the creatures of the earth to a second Noah's Ark, the only word he would have for the motion of each kind would be, "go".

So "cabined, cribbed, confined" is he in the knowledge of words that of this mighty spectacle he could make nothing. But put into the working vocabulary of this single-verbed speaker creep and crawl, flutter and fly, pace and patter, shuffle and shamble, run and race, amble and antic, wobble and waltz, leap and loiter, lilt and limp, flit and flounder, prance and plod, hop and hurry along, skip and skelp, tread and troop, march and meander— supplant the paucity of his vocabulary with words such as these, and then he might observe the variety of the spectacle.

—J. Frank Dobie, "Words, Words, Words, My Lord"[2]

However adept we may be at using words, they are always off-the-shelf items. We don't get to impose our private meanings on them. Rather they impose their meanings on us. They frame and color our reality just as they give us the wherewithal "to observe the variety of the spectacle."

The fact is that the use of words is a compromise, or more to the point, our *thoughts* are being compromised. By using a particular word, we concede to its consensus meaning and all the baggage packed into it, none of which was provided by us—its history, its emotional associations, and its biases. "We believe that we know something about the things themselves," Neitszche observed, "when we speak of trees, colors, snow, and flowers; and yet we possess nothing but metaphors for things—metaphors which correspond in no way to the original entities."[3]

The communal property of language—available to express thoughts that are ostensibly *original* to the individual—is a powerful force for ensuring conformity in a culture. The power of words to *create* our perception cannot be overstated. Aldous Huxley, who gave us *Brave New World*, elsewhere observed, "'A mere matter of words', we say contemptuously, forgetting that words have the power to mould men's thinking, to canalize their feeling, to direct their willing and acting. Conduct and character are largely determined by the nature of the words we currently use to discuss ourselves and the world around us."[4]

The view that language profoundly affects perception, intuited by Huxley and countless others, was first formally developed as a hypothesis by Benjamin Lee Whorf and Edward Sapir in the 1920s and 30s. Whorf's landmark book *Language, Thought and Reality* gave rise to the field of general semantics, and by now its core principle seems self-evident. Sapir articulates it clearly,

> Human beings do not live in the objective world alone, not alone in the world of social activity as ordinarily understood, but are very much at the mercy of the particular language which has become the medium of expression for their society. It is quite an illusion to imagine that one adjusts to reality essentially without the use of language and that language is merely an incidental means of solving particular problems of communication or reflection. The fact of the matter is that the "real world" is to a large extent unconsciously built up on the language habits of the group ... We see and hear and otherwise experience very largely as we do because the language habits of our community predispose certain choices of interpretation.
>
> —Edward Sapir, "The Status of Linguistic Science in America"[5]

Language imposes a way of seeing. We are not in command of language nearly as much as we may imagine. Language is in command of us by providing us with a prefabricated model with which to *think*. This phenomenon has not been underappreciated by those who would manipulate the reality of others for power. It is the first principle of tyrants.

To corrupt reality, one need only be successful in corrupting language. A corrupt or distorted reality *requires* corrupted language to exist. In Orwell's novel *1984*, which introduced "Big Brother" into our language, the protagonist, Winston Smith, works in the Ministry of Truth. The Ministry of Truth, of course, produces anything *but* the truth. Winston works there because of his proficiency in writing "newspeak." Newspeak is a new language designed to impose Big Brother's alternative reality of oppression. It does so by introducing new words and phasing out of old words found in "Oldspeak." The diabolical nature of newspeak was to retain familiar words but eradicate their undesirable meanings and associations. Orwell describes the process early in the novel,

> The purpose of Newspeak was not only to provide a medium of expression for the world view and mental habits of the devotees of Ingsoc, [English Socialists] but to make all other modes of thought impossible. It was intended that when Newspeak had been adopted once and for all and Oldspeak forgotten, a heretical thought ... should be literally unthinkable, at least as far as thought is dependent on words ... This was done partly by the invention of new words, but chiefly by eliminating undesirable words and by stripping such words as remained of un-orthodox meanings, and so far as possible of all secondary meanings whatever.

> To give a single example. The word "free" still existed in Newspeak, but it could only be used in such statements as "This dog is free of lice," or "This field is free of weeds." It could not be used in its old sense of "politically free" or "intellectually free" since political and intellectual freedom no longer existed even as concepts, and were therefore of necessity nameless... Newspeak was designed not to extend but to diminish the range of thought, and this purpose was assisted by cutting the choice of words down to a minimum.

> —George Orwell, *1984*[6]

Orwell imagined a totalitarian society in which language was designed and manipulated from a central controlling authority. But the effect of language and the invention of Newspeak is as prevalent in *free* societies. The principal difference is that in a free society—especially one like ours that has become addicted to the democratized cacophony of the Internet—Newspeak is not centrally managed but appears everywhere. Who among us has not been affected in one way or another by the invention of the term *death panel* to displace *a right to voluntary counseling on end-of-life issues*? How many of us have either been dismayed or heartened by the use of the word *regime* to refer to a presidential *administration* or by the new compulsion to modify the word *policy* with adjectives such as *socialist* or *fascist* or *un-American* or even *insane*?

Language is organic. It changes all the time—literally as we speak. However, the intensity of the assault on language itself, the conscious effort to debase the currency of words for purposes having little to do with honest expression, rises and falls with the political or social barometer.

As consequential as this process is in shaping our world, it is mostly hidden in plain sight. It is subtle and insidious. We can be excused if we are not as attuned to the effects of language on our perceptions and on the nature of our reality until their impact is impossible to ignore as when the language of medicine and illness suddenly become a formative part of our lives.

"You have Parkinson's disease" is as traumatic a set of words as anyone is likely to hear in a lifetime. In my case, there was an attempt by the physician to mitigate the impact of the news. He said, "I think you have a *touch* of Parkinson's." I remember thinking at the time, *As in a touch of class or a touch of the flu?* I couldn't reconcile *touch of* with *Parkinson's disease*. A missile of sorts had just been aimed at my head, and the doctor's choice of words was trying to turn it into a cotton ball. The effort fell short. The term *Parkinson's disease* is far too weaponized to be defused by a mere *touch of.* The diagnosis of Parkinson's disease, uttered like a verdict of *guilty*, signaled not just the start of a medical odyssey but the navigation of a new world of words.

What is it that we think of when we think of Parkinson's? And how close to the truth of it is the language we use? Is it a *disease* or an *illness* or a *disorder*?

A *disease* has the air of permanence about it, of something having taken root deep within ourselves. A *disease* is serious business; it requires a *cure*.

An *illness*, on the other hand, carries with it the feel of a temporary state. One stays home from work when one is *ill*, and if suddenly we're *taken ill*, the prospect of recovery is implicit.

And of the three terms, the most benign seems to be *disorder*. Although *disorder* can suggest chaos, *order* is something that is often *restored*. It's just that for a while things have been thrown out of sorts, but they might eventually be righted. It is telling that the administrative assistants at the Neurological Institute of New York's Presbyterian Hospital answer the phone by saying, "Department of Movement *Disorders*" as opposed to saying, "Department of Movement *Diseases*."

The language of disease is never felicitous. A word such as *affliction*, for example, suggests an assault from outside the body (as does *stricken*), and *sickness* pretty much relegates those who are afflicted to linguistic purgatory.

Disease is frightening, and there is no avoiding the fact that language will reflect this ... and should. Otherwise, we would be delusional. On the other hand, the language associated with Parkinson's disease is especially onerous but perhaps needlessly so. Parkinson's is a notoriously heterogeneous disease. It affects different people in dramatically different ways, and the varieties of medication often cause sharply contrasting and sometimes unpredictable side effects in patients. Yet the language of Parkinson's—as is the language of disease in general—tends to homogenize the experience. The resulting impression may be that if you've seen one Parkinson's patient, you've seen them all. Two of the culprits are *progressive* and *degenerative,* often expressed in tandem as in one saying, "Parkinson's is a *progressive, degenerative* neurological disease."

Progressive is a notoriously inexact term. Yet when it is uttered in a scientific and medical context, it takes on the bias of exactitude. *Progressive* is roughly equivalent in meaning to *advancing* but suggests nothing of rate or speed or magnitude. All we know is that Parkinson's has forward motion, but without further details, the *progress* may occur at a gallop or a snail's pace.

Degenerative is an ominous word denoting a process of *disintegration*, the end result of which is nothingness. Physiologically, the actual breakdown has to do with nerve cells and chemical interactivity, but the word suggests a journey of indeterminate duration toward total dissolution.

These meanings are likely not what our physician would have us think about when we think of Parkinson's. But language frames what reality it will, and by its nature, it is a difficult beast to tame in spite of our efforts. It is hard enough in *normal* life to resist the conformities or distortions language naturally invests in us. With the onset of *illnesses* or *diseases* or *disorders*—or whatever imprecise descriptors we are most comfortable in using—the challenge is greater because the stakes are higher. If we allow *progressive* to impose a reality upon us that is *rampant* rather *incremental* or *measured* or even *slow*, we confer unchecked power to words that perhaps is not deserved and often does us no good. If we allow *degenerative* to extend its meaning beyond microscopic cells and neurological structures to include the whole of ourselves and our lives, we needlessly add an accelerant to the process.

Those of us living with Parkinson's and chronic neurological diseases must put up with biases of language that sometimes make our circumstances less tolerable. Familiar words like *shuffle* and *frozen* and *shake* and *gait* lose some of their Oldspeak meanings and take on new signification in our unbidden new world. It is important to be conscious of the shift and appreciate the fact that language and words are not neutral bystanders of our social interplay and personal reflections. Yet however powerful a force they may be in coloring our reality, we are not entirely defenseless in resisting their imprecision and misrepresentations of our individual experience. We are empowered by recognizing that words are always surrogates. The word is never the thing.

CHAPTER 25

The Future

Georgia O'Keefe, "The Beyond", Georgia O'Keefe
Museum, Santa Fe/Art Resource, NY

For I dipt into the future, far as human eye could see,
Saw the vision of the world, and all the wonder that would be;
Saw the heavens fill with commerce, argosies of magic sails,
Pilots of the purple twilight, dropping down with costly bales;
Heard the heavens fill with shouting, and there rain'd a ghastly dew
From the nations' airy navies grappling in the central blue;
Far along the world-wide whisper of the south-wind rushing warm,

With the standards of the peoples plunging thro' the thunder-storm;
Till the war-drum throbbed no longer, and the battle-flags were furl'd
In the Parliament of man, the Federation of the world.
There the common sense of most shall hold a fretful realm in awe,
And the kindly earth shall slumber, lapt in universal law.
So I triumph'd, ere my passion sweeping thro' me left me dry,
Left me with the palsied heart, and left me with the jaundiced eye.

—Alfred Lord Tennyson, from *Locksley Hall*[1]

When in the spring a robin is moved to build her nest in preparation for the hatching of her chicks, she does so literally without a thought. As far as science can tell, the robin has no notion whatever about what she's doing or why. There are no visions of chirping newborns dancing in her head, no plan. There is only instinctive behavior—a series of unconnected moments one after the other like beads on a string. The robin lives with no idea of past or future as does every creature on earth with the possible exception of a few higher primates and the certain exception of man.

For us, the past and the future are always *here*. Life is one long present moment colored by what has come before and what we imagine might follow. Walt Whitman, who was as much a poet of the future as any who ever lived, understood that we live in a nexus of overlapping time. In his introduction to *Leaves of Grass*, he writes,

> Past, present and future are not disjoined but joined. The greatest poet forms the consistence of what is to be from what has been and is. He drags the dead out of their coffins and stands them again on their feet … He says to the past, Rise and walk before me that I can realize you. He learns the lesson … he places himself where the future becomes present.

—Walt Whitman, *Leaves of Grass*[2]

In his typically provocative fashion, Whitman reverses the relationship between the present and the future. Rather than state the obvious—that the present somehow creates the future—he declares that "the future *becomes* the present," and so it does, especially for those of us who are concerned more so than others with what lies ahead. How will our illness progress? What will life be like a year from now … or five? Will a cure for Parkinson's disease be found? When? The questions themselves and the things imagined—whether hopeful or despairing—are not a part of the future at all. They are a part of our present, and even when they become actualized, it will be the present then too.

Yet it is difficult for us not to view the future as separate and apart from our current experience and still ahead. *What does the future hold?* is a preeminent human question. Prophets, seers, and sorcerers have always been with us to provide us with answers, and we've proved that we cannot resist their mystical intensity. We almost never fail to assume that knowing the future is a means to greater personal power or affords us the chance to escape an unwelcome or untimely fate. It is for this reason that peculiar flights of birds have countless times changed the course of history.

Yet as much as we desire to know what the future holds, the more haunting question—or even the more interesting one—is as follows: *If it were possible to know what the future holds, is it best for us to know or not to know?*

With respect to our physical world, the answer is obvious and not troubling. We can only benefit from knowing future outcomes. If I turn the wheel of my car sharply to the left, I will avoid the oncoming truck. If such and such drug is administered at such and such dosage, it will result in a cure a certain percentage of the time. If an airliner reaches a groundspeed of 267 mile per hour, it will lift off the runway and fly. And the list goes on. Predictive reliability is the foundation of the physical sciences.

In the case of our individual futures, however, the answer of whether or not foreknowledge is a good thing is far less straightforward. The historical and literary record suggests that human beings are not only notoriously inaccurate in predicting future events, but when we do think we know what is coming, we often behave badly—impulsively, maniacally, irrationally, fearfully, arrogantly. We almost cannot resist leveraging what we know, deriving maximum gain from it or in some way changing it to better suit our purposes.

Most of us, I suspect, have asked our physicians for a prognosis about our condition. It is a rare person who, upon being diagnosed with a serious illness, refrains from asking. And of course, we are familiar with the common response—guarded, noncommittal, and respectful of the limitations of medical science and the role of chance.

The best physicians know—and we would be well advised to acknowledge it as well—that predictions diminish our capacity to imagine *possibilities*, and possibilities are essential to hopefulness. Knowing the future may also introduce moral choices for which we might be ill-prepared or reluctant to make, as might be the case with a woman upon learning the results of her amniocenteses or when one's genetic predisposition to certain diseases has been mapped.

The future hardly ever evolves into the present without irony or unexpected consequences. This has been the case with monumental events in human history as well as in the truths of high art. Attention ought to be paid.

If we accept that the future is never fixed but materializes from among infinite preceding possibilities that are themselves not predetermined, then we accept a world of free will and free action. Anything can happen. On the other hand, if we perceive the future to be fixed, altering it would be a logical impossibility. It cannot be both mutable *and* the future. This truth seems to have eluded many consequential actors in history as well as some of the most compelling characters in fiction.

In Western culture there is hardly a more consequential example of an attempt to alter the future than what has come to be called the Massacre of the Innocents. As told in Matthew 2:1–23, Herod the Great ruled Judea at the time of Christ's birth. Wise men "from the east" came to Jerusalem and inquired, "Where is he that is born King of the Jews?"[3] Disturbed by the news that a child had been born in Bethlehem who was prophesied to usurp his throne, Herod instructed the wise men to visit the child and report back so that Herod himself might visit and worship Him. An angel appeared to Joseph, instructing him to take Mary and the child and flee to Egypt. The wise men were warned in a dream not to obey Herod and to return home. In a rage about being deceived by the magi, Herod ordered the massacre of the male infants of Bethlehem in an effort to defeat the prophecy.

> Then Herod, when he saw that he was mocked by the wise men, was exceeding wroth, and sent forth, and slew all the children that were in Bethlehem, and in all the coasts thereof, from two years old and under, according to the time which he had diligently inquired of the wise men.
>
> —The Holy Bible, Matthew[4]

Herod wielded absolute power over Judea, power that was derived in turn from Rome itself. Yet despite his efforts, the Christ child escaped as did the wise men. The future is unalterable.

In Sophocles's *Oedipus the King*, the same truth is confirmed in even more dramatic fashion. After learning from an oracle that he is destined to die at the hands of his own son, King Laius orders his wife, Queen Jocasta, to kill their infant. Instead she entrusts the task to a servant who cannot bear to murder the boy and so abandons him in the wilderness. He is found by a shepherd, and eventually, the infant is adopted by the childless king and queen of Corinth who name him Oedipus.

As a young man, Oedipus suspects that the royal couple are not his biological parents and consults the Delphic oracle. Although the oracle does not answer the question relating to Oedipus's adoption, it prophecies that Oedipus will kill his father and marry his mother. Horrified at the prospect and believing that the king and queen are indeed his true parents, Oedipus leaves Corinth for Thebes lest he harm them.

On the road to Thebes, he quarrels with a stranger and kills him. Soon after, he solves the riddle of the Sphinx, which has held a curse over Thebes, and is rewarded with marriage to the widowed Queen Jocasta. All of this, of course, ends badly. Powerful taboos have been broken, and the world needs to be set right. Oedipus blinds himself so that he may no longer experience the abomination of laying eyes on his children begotten with his own mother, and Jocasta hangs herself. The future, once fixed, cannot be evaded.[5]

Just as the future proves itself unalterable, a prophecy—even if true—often turns out to be very different than first supposed. Macbeth is emboldened by a string of prophecies he receives from three witches. He will soon become Thane of Cawdor and then king.[6] "None of woman born shall harm [him]," and he "shall never vanquished be until/Great Birnan wood to high Dunsinane hill/shall come against him,"[7] fortified by these seemingly incontrovertible assurances and the steely resolve of Lady Macbeth,

Macbeth murders his way to the Scottish crown. Yet he is ultimately defeated by Macduff, whose army advances upon Macbeth on Dunsinane hill while camouflaged with vegetation from Birnan wood and who kills Macbeth as he reveals to him that he was born by Caesarian section and "from his mother's womb untimely ripped."[8]

In *Macbeth*, Shakespeare demonstrates with tragic irony the foolhardiness of assuming that our understanding of the future can ever be complete or that we can reliably know the nature of our destiny before it is upon us. However well-calculated our present choices might be and however confidently we might anticipate their consequences, the future invariably carries its own surprises. This would seem to apply as readily to the seizing of a throne as it would to the outcome of a progressive illness.

Uncertainty is the constant, and irony is inevitable. Yet we never seem to tire of trying to rid ourselves of these troublesome elements of life. We strive for greater certainty and often convince ourselves into believing that we have it within our grasp. This might explain why so many people diagnosed with serious illness immediately race to their computers to learn all there is to know about it and what the future holds. It is an all-too-human impulse to believe that information is power, that knowledge is control. It is sometimes the case, of course but often it is an illusion.

Our desire to believe in an orderly universe leads us to believe that the uncertainty we feel about the future as nothing but the consequence of our current state of ignorance to be dispelled by greater knowledge or better analysis. But even a modest amount of randomness can play havoc with our intuitions. Because it is always possible, after the fact, to come up with a story about why things worked out the way they did—that the first "Harry Potter" really was a brilliant book, even if the eight publishers who rejected it didn't know it at the time—our belief in determinism is rarely shaken, no matter how often we are surprised. But just because we now know that something happened doesn't imply that we could have known it was going to happen at the time, even in principle, because at the time, it wasn't going to necessarily happen at all.

—Duncan J. Watts [9]

We long for certainty and are forever vexed by our shortcomings and the unpredictability of life, especially the suddenness of its catastrophes. But this is not necessarily cause for despair. "The imperfect is our paradise," writes Wallace Stevens, and "in this bitterness, delight .../Lies in flawed words and stubborn sounds."[10]

But how can delight lie in the imperfect?

The answer may be because in the imperfect—in a present of great struggle or in a future that is unknowable—there remain *possibilities*. There are no possibilities in certainty and perfection. The possibilities have been exhausted. It is the existence of possibilities that allows human beings to breathe and the "never-resting mind" to imagine. The end of possibilities is the end of hope and the beginning of some sort of existence other than the one we recognize as human. It is in the best works of science fiction, and in the hands of our greatest writers of that genre, we explore the consequences of alternative futures and the blurry line between human and nonhuman capacities. In Frank Herbert's *God Emperor of Dune*, the emperor Leto possesses the power to know the future but "comes to understand that life must be evolutionary and characterized by choice and chance, even though this may not be what people, blinded by the crisis of the moment, want."[11] Philip K. Dick's "precogs"—mutants with the capability of precognition or knowing what is to happen before it happens—are nonhuman in the sense that they robotically follow the path of the inevitable.[12]

Certainty may be our passion, but it is not our gift.

Epilogue

In writing this book, I have tried to make a small contribution to the community of those who are living with Parkinson's disease and other serious illnesses. My approach has been deliberately oblique, but I hope it has also been compelling enough for each reader to derive some benefit. My aim has been to remain as dispassionate as possible. At this point, though, I am inclined to take some liberties.

By any yardstick, Parkinson's disease is a calamity. It is an assault on the body and mind at the foundational level—an assault on movement, which we depend upon *to act*, and on memory, which we depend upon *to think*. It need not also be an assault on our spirit.

Of the people I have met in connection with this project, especially those whom I have interviewed, every one without exception has refused to relent to Parkinson's disease. They have turned the illness on itself, absorbing its insults but somehow transforming its negative force into strength. They endure what they must and summon courage enough when they need it.

It has been a great pleasure to revisit or read for the first time great literary work or to reflect on important art, and I hope readers have been moved to do the same themselves. But in traveling this terrain, what has struck me most has been the resilience of human beings when faced with the impossible or the unimaginable or the inexpressible. They—*we*—seem to find a way to display the uniquely human quality of dignity in spite of its elusiveness in our accidental community of Parkinson's disease.

As indicated from the start, my purpose has been modest. I have offered no answers. Nor have I served as an advocate for any particular point of view. I have provided only grist for the mill. The great questions—*What is it all about? Why is life the way it is? What does it all mean?*—have remained predictably unanswered.

But not everything is a mystery. Not everything means nothing as some would have us believe. Each of us is, after all, a human being whose very existence defies odds too enormous to contemplate and who is alive and aware amidst a vast, indifferent and insensate infinitude. Regardless of what may have befallen us and what may yet come, ours is already a great triumph.

> I am the eye with which the Universe
> Beholds itself and knows itself divine;
> All harmony of instrument or verse,
> All prophecy, all medicine is mine,
> All light of art or nature—to my song
> Victory and praise in its own right belong.

—Percy Bysshe Shelley, *Hymn of Apollo*[1]

Endnotes

Preface

1. Virginia Woolf, *Mrs. Dalloway* 1925 (New York: Alfred A. Knopf, Everyman's Library: 1993), 87–88.
2. Susan Sontag, *Illness as Metaphor and AIDS and Its Metaphors* (New York: Farrar, Strauss and Giroux, 1990), 3–4.
3. Joseph Campbell (with Bill Moyers), ed. Betty Sue Flowers, *The Power of Myth* (New York: Doubleday, 1988), 10.
4. Peter J. Gomes, *The Good Book: Reading the Bible with Mind and Heart* (New York: William Morrow and Company, Inc., 1996), 214.
5. _____, 215.
6. Emily Dickinson, "By a departing light" in *The Complete Poems of Emily Dickinson*, ed. Thomas H. Johnson. (Boston: Little, Brown and Company, 1960), 1714.
7. Anatole Broyard, *Intoxicated by My Illness* (New York: Ballantine Books, 1992), *passim*.

Chapter 1

1. William Blake, "The Tyger" in *The Complete Poetry and Prose of William Blake*, ed. David V. Erdman (Berkeley: University of California Berkeley Press, 1982), 25.
2. Joseph Conrad, *Lord Jim* (Norwalk: Easton Press, 1977), 8–9.
3. Ecclesiastes 9:11 (KJV).
4. _____, Job 1:6–7.
5. _____, Job 1:8.
6. _____, Genesis 22:1–19.
7. _____, Genesis 3:10.

Chapter 2

1. Herman Melville, *Moby Dick* or *The White Whale* (Norwalk: Easton Press, 1977), 171.

2   _____, 174.

3   Tobi Zausner, "When Walls Become Doorways," *Creativity Research Journal* 11 (1998): 21.

4   Robert Frost, from "Reluctance," *The Poetry of Robert Frost*, ed. Edward Connery Latham (New York: Henry Holt and Company, 1969), 30.

5   John Milton, *Paradise Lost* (Norwalk: Easton Press, 1976), book I, 9.

6   Alan Watts, *The Way of Zen* (New York: Pantheon, 1989), ix.

7   Sontag, 6–7.

8   Pima Chodron, *When Things Fall Apart* (New York: Shambala, 1997), 8.

9   _____, 9.

10   Campbell, 161.

Chapter 3

1   William Wordsworth, from "Ode: Intimations of Immortality on Recollections of Childhood," *The Complete Poetical Works of William Wordsworth*, Cambridge edition, ed. Andrew J. George (New York: Houghton Mifflin Company, 1904), 353–54.

2   Kris Kristofferson, "The Pilgrim: Chapter 33," *The Essential Kris Kristofferson* (SONY BMG, 2004).

3   Aeschylus, "Agamemnon," *The Complete Greek Tragedies, Vol. 1: Aeschylus*, ed. David Greene and Richmond Lattimore (Chicago: University of Chicago Press, 1991), 42, ll, 250–54.

4   Adalet Baris Gunersel, "Dionysian Frenzy—Myth or Reality?" *American Creativity Association Annual Conference* 2005. Austin, TX.

5   Zausner, 22.

6   _____, 21.

7   Harold Bloom, *Genius: A Mosaic of One Hundred Exemplary Creative Minds* (New York: Warner Books, 2002), 323.

8   _____, *passim*.

9   Wordsworth, 355–56, X.

10   Bloom, *passim*.

11   Wordsworth, 356, XI.

Chapter 4

1   Horace, "Odes" trans. Michel de Montaigne in "To Think as a Philosopher is to Learn to Die," *The Essays of Michel de Montaigne*, trans. George B. Ives (New York: The Heritage Press, 1946), 117.

2   Plato, "Socrates' Defense (Apology)," *Plato: The Collected Dialogues*, trans. Edith Hamilton and Huntington Cairns. Bolingen Series LXXI (Princeton: Princeton University Press, 1996), 4.

3 Ernest Hemingway, *For Whom the Bell Tolls* (Shelton, CT: First Edition Library: 1968), 471.

4 William Shakespeare, "Macbeth," *The Riverside Shakespeare*, eds. G. Blakemore Evans et. al. (Boston: Houghton Mifflin Company, 1974), I, vii, ll, 54–61.

5 Rollo May, *The Courage to Create* (New York: W.W. Norton and Company, Inc., 1975), 12.

Chapter 5

1 Miguel de Cervantes, *Don Quixote*, trans. Edith Grossman (New York: Harper Collins Publishers, 2004), 59.

2 Michel de Montaigne, as cited in Charles Rosen, "The Genius of Montaigne," *The New York Review of Books* 14 (Feb. 2008): 53.

3 Cervantes, 666.

Chapter 6

1 Samuel Taylor Coleridge, "Kubla Kahn: A Fragment," The Norton Anthology of English Literature, 2nd edition, vol. 2., ed. M. H. Abrams et. al. (New York: W. W. Norton & Company, 2000), 439.

2 Thomas Moore, *The Re-Enchantment of Everyday Life* (New York: HarperCollins Publishers, 1996), ix.

3 _____, xvii.

4 Blake, "The Book of Thel: Thel's Motto," 3.

5 Stephen Sondheim, from *Pacific Overtures*.

6 Dickinson, Emily. *The Complete Poems of Emily Dickinson*, ed. Thomas H. Johnson (Boston: Little, Brown and Company, 1960). See "There's a certain slant of light…"

7 Alfred Lord Tennyson, from "The Lady of Shalott," *The Norton Anthology of English Literature*, 2nd edition, vol. 2. ed. M. H. Abrams (New York: W. W. Norton & Company, 2000), 1,204.

8 W. B. Yeats, from "The Wild Swans at Coole," *The Complete Collected Works of W. B. Yeats: Volume I: The Poems*, ed. Richard J. Finnerman (New York: Scribner, 1983), 131.

9 Joseph Conrad, *The Shadow Line: A Confession* (New York: Vintage Books, 2007), 129.

Chapter 7

1 Joseph Conrad, *Heart of Darkness* (New York: Alfred A. Knopf, 1993), 37.

2 Fyodor Dostoevsky, *The Brothers Karamazov* (New York: Alfred A. Knopf, 1990), chapters 1, 2, *passim*.

3   Albert Camus, *The Stranger*, trans. Matthew Ward (New York: Alfred A. Knopf, 1993), 1.

4   Rabbi Hillel, as cited in Harold Bloom, *Where Shall Wisdom be Found?* (New York: Riverhead Books, 2004), 5.

5   T. S. Eliot, from "The Loves Song of J. Alfred Proofrock," *The Waste Land* (New York: Harcourt, Brace and Company, 1936), 11.

Chapter 8

1   James Joyce, *The Dubliners* (New York: Alfred A. Knopf, 1967), 118.

2   Homer, *The Iliad*, trans.Robert Fagles (New York: Viking, 1990). book III, ll, 216–19.

3   Plato, *The Republic*, book VII, 747.

4   _____, 749.

Chapter 9

1   Alan Lightman, *Einstein's Dreams* (New York: Pantheon Books, 1993), 174–75.

2   John Keats, "Ode on a Grecian Urn," *The Odes of John Keats*, ed. Helen Vendler (Cambridge: The Belknap Press of Harvard University Press, 1983), 114–15.

3   Cormac McCarthy, *The Road* (New York: Alfred A. Knopf, 2006), 241.

4   Stanley Kunitz, *The Collected Poems* (New York: Norton, 2005), 1.

5   Karel Capek, *The Makropoulos Affair*.

6   _____.

7   Lucius Seneca, *On the Shortness of Life*, trans. C. D. N. Costa (New York: Penguin Books, 1997), 1–2.

Chapter 10

1   Wallace Stevens, "The Poems of Our Climate," *American Poetry: The 20th Century*, vol. I, Advisory Board: Robert Hass et. al. (New York: The Library of America, 2000), 315.

2   Moriarty, Sheila; Fasulo, John; Bissell, Patricia; Curfman, April; Thompson, Peter; Warford, Pam; Grandoff, Nancy; Iverson, Dave. Telephone interviews with this author, December 2009–January 2010.

3   Samuel Beckett, *Malone Dies* (New York: Grove Press, 1956), 16.

4   May, 39.

5   _____, 25.

6   _____, 54.

7   _____, 41.

8   Phillip Sandblom, *Creativity and Disease* (London: Marion Boyars Publishers, 2009), 167.

9   *Velasquez*, eds. Antonio Dominguez Ortiz et. al., foreword by Philippe de Montebello, director (New York: The Metropolitan Museum of Art and Harry N. Abrams, Inc., 1989), ix.

10   _____.

11   The Metropolitan Museum of Art, gallery label: "Juan de Pareja" by Velazquez.

12   Moriarty.

13   Fasulo.

14   John Ruskin, as cited by Arthur C. Danto, "The Unknown Masterpiece by Honore de Balzac," *Unkown Masterpieces*, ed. Edwin Frank (New York: New York Review of Books, 2003), 21.

15   Frost, "Birches," 121.

16   JackieBarzeley, Parkinson's Disease Foundation website, "The Gallery Poetry/Writing," 2007.

17   Robert Canning, Parkinson's Disease Foundation website, "The Gallery Poetry/Writing."

18   John King, unpublished.

19   Trish Bissell, Parkinson's Disease Foundation website, "The Gallery Poetry/Writing."

20   Keats, "Endymion," *The Complete Poems of John Keats* (New York: The Modern Library, 1994), 47.

21   Nathaniel West, *Miss Lonelyhearts & The Day of the Locust* (New York: Modern Library Edition, 1998), 7.

Chapter 11

1   Lewis Carroll, *Alice's Adventures in Wonderland* (Norwalk, CT: Easton Press, 1977), 59–60.

2   Alexander Solzhenitsyn, *The Cancer Ward* (New York: Farrar, Straus and Giroux, 1969), 10.

3, 4, 5, 6 Vladimir Nabokov, "The Metamorphosis," *Lectures on Literature*, ed. Fredson Bowers (San Diego: Harcourt, Inc., 1980) as transcribed online at: http://victorian.fortunecity.com/vermeer/287/nabokov_s_metamorphosis.htm. (No page numbers accompanied electronic text.)

7   William Barrett, *Irrational Man: A Study in Existential Philosophy* (Garden City, NY: Doubleday Anchor Books, 1958), 196.

8   _____.

9   Campbell, 193.

10   Shakespeare, *King Lear*, I, i, ll, 294.

11   _____, I, i, ll, 92–93.

12   _____, I, iv, ll, 288–89.

13   _____, II, iv, ll, 147–51.

14   _____, III, ii, ll, 14–21.

[15] _____, III, ii, ll, 59–60.

[16] _____, III, iv, ll, 21–2.

[17] _____, III, iv, 32–33.

[18] _____, III, iv, ll, 105–8.

[19] Jean-Paul Sartre, "The Flies," *No Exit and Three Other Plays* (New York: Alfred A. Knopf, 1976), act III, 119.

[20] _____, IV, vii, 83–84.

[21] _____, V, iii, ll, 8–18.

[22] Montaigne, "Of Experience," 1,518.

[23] _____.

[24] Virginia Woolf, *The Common Reader*, first series (London: Hogarth Press, 1962), 86.

Chapter 12

[1] F. Scott Fitzgerald, *The Great Gatsby* (Shelton, CT: First Edition Library, 1953), 217–18.

[2] Hemingway, 169.

[3] Vladimir Nabakov, *Speak, Memory* (New York: Everyman's Library, Alfred A. Knopf, 1999).

[4] James Joyce, *A Portrait of the Artist as a Young Man* (New York: Everyman's Library, Alfred A. Knopf, 1991), 82–84.

[5] Woolf, 287.

[6] Ralph Waldo Emerson, "History," *Essays*, first series (New York: BiblioBazaar, 2009), 13.

[7] Phyllis Rose, *The Year of Reading Proust* (New York: Scribner's, 1997), 27.

[8] Saul Bellow, *Ravelstein* (New York: Viking, 2000), 192.

[9] C. V. Cavafy, "Ithaca," *The Complete Poems of Cavafy*, trans. Rae Dalven (New York: Harcourt, Brace & World, Inc., 1948), 36.

Chapter 13

[1] Conrad, 308.

[2] Raymond Carver, "Fear," *Where Water Comes Together with Other Water* (New York: Random House, 1985), 12.

[3] Shakespeare, King Lear, V, ii, ll, 9–11.

[4] Harold B. Simpson, *Audie Murphy: American Soldier* (Texas: Alcor Publishing Company, 1985), 369–71.

[5] Homer, book 22, ll, 157–65; 171–72.

[6] Genesis 3:10.

[7] Campbell, 115.

8   Seamus Heaney, *Beowulf: A New Version Translation by Seamus Heaney* (New York: Farrar, Strauss and Giroux, 1999) ll, 814–26.

Chapter 14

1   Homer, *The Odyssey*, trans. Robert Fagles (New York: Viking, 1996), book VI, ll, 198–203.

2   Mortimer J. Adler, "Happiness," *The Great Ideas: A Lexicon of Western Thought* (New York: Scribner Classics, 1992), 296.

3   Gregg Easterbrook, *The Progress Paradox* (New York: Random House, 2003), 166.

4   Bellow, *Herzog* (New York: The Viking Press, 1964), 1.

5   John Locke, "An Essay Concerning Human Understanding," digitized Google e-book, 171–72.

6   Adler, 296.

7   Easterbrook, *Passim*.

8   Easterbrook, 164.

9   _____, 165.

10   _____.

11   Oscar Wilde, "The Portrait of Mr. W. H.," *The Short Stories of Oscar Wilde* (Norwalk: The Easton Press, 1976), 20–21.

12   D. H. Lawrence, "The Rocking Horse Winner," *The Oxford Book of Short Stories* (New York: Oxford University Press, 1981), 275–90.

13   Leo Tolstoy, *Anna Karenina*, trans. Constance (Norwalk: Easton Press, 1975), 1.

14   Yeats, from "Man and the Echo," 353.

Chapter 15

1   Eliot, from "The Burial of the Dead," *The Waste Land*, 70.

2   W. H. Auden, "Herman Melville," in *Melville*, 146.

3   *The Oxford Classical Dictionary*, 3rd edition, eds. Simon Hornblower and Antony Spawforth (New York: Oxford University Press, 1996), 521.

4   *The Book of the Dead: The Hieroglyphic Transcript and Translation into English of the Ancient Egyptian Papyrus of Ani*, commentary by E.A. Wallis Budge (New York: Gramercy Books, 1994), 76, 130.

5   John 3:24, 25.

6   Nabakov, 1.

7   James Boswell, *The Life of Samuel Johnson* (New York: Alfred A. Knopf, 1992), 12.

8   Eliot, "Burnt Norton," *The Waste Land*, 214.

9   Harold Bloom, *Hamlet: Poem Unlimited* (New York: Riverhead Books, 2007), *passim*.

10   Shakespeare, *Hamlet*, V, ii, 219–24.
11   Marcus Aurelius, *Meditations*, trans. Maxwell Staniforth (New York: Dorset Press, 1986), 179.
12   Ecclesiastes 3:20.
13   *The New York Times Guide to Essential Knowledge*, ed. John W. Wright (New York: St. Martin's Press, 2004), 439.
14   Ronald Bailey, *Liberation Biology: The Scientific and Moral Case for the Biotech Revolution* (Amherst, NY: Prometheus Books: 2005), 15.
15   Bailey, "Forever Young," *Reason Magazine* (August/September 2002).
16   Francis Fukuyama, *Our Posthuman Future: Consequences of the Biotechnology Revolution* (New York: Picador, 2005), *passim*.
17   Bailey, 19.
18   Heaney, "What Passed at Colonus," *New York Review of Books* LL, no. 15 (October 7, 2004): 14.

Chapter 16

1   Mark 9:42–49.
2   Heaney, "What Passed at Colonus."
3   The Gallup Organization, "Values and Beliefs Survey" as cited by Albert N. Winsman, *Commentary Magazine* (May 2004).
4   _____.
5   Jonathan Edwards, "Sinners in the Hands of an Angry God," a sermon preached in Enfield, CT (July 8, 1741), *American Sermons* (New York: The Library of America, 1999), 353–54.
6   Milton, book I, 3.
7   _____.
8   Gallup.
9   Dante's hell, http://padresteve.files.wordpress.com/2010/02/danteinferno_400x606.jpg.
10   Michael Cunningham, *The Hours* (New York: Farrar, Strauss and Giroux, 1998), 167
11   Milton, book I, 9.
13   Phyllis W. Rose, "The Poet's Heaven," *Gentlemen's Magazine* CCLXXXVI (June–September 1899): 39.

Chapter 17

1   Homer, *The Iliad*, book 9, ll, 497–505.
2   Revelation 1:8.
3   Job 13:15

4   St. Augustine, *De Libero Arbitrio* as cited in F. Anne Payne's "Foreknowledge and Free Will: Three Theories in the Nun's Priest's Tale," *The Chaucer Review* 10, no. 3 (Winter 1976): 201–9.

5   Bernard Knox, "Introduction," Homer, *The Iliad*, 5.

6   Sophocles, "Oedipus the King," *The Complete Greek Tragedies*, vol. II, 71, ll, 1,370–77.

7   _____, 76, ll, 1,524–30.

Chapter 18

1   Dickinson, "Hope is the thing with feathers," 254.

2   Karl Meninger, "The Academic Lecture on Hope," *The Journal of American Psychiatry* (December 1959): 484.

3   _____, 483.

4   F. Scott Fitzgerald, *The Great Gatsby* (Shelton, CT: First Edition Library, 1953), 217–18.

5   _____, 133.

6   Hemingway, "Fathers and Sons," *The Nick Adams Stories* (New York: Scribner, 1972), 258.

7   Heaney. *The Cure at Troy: A Version of Sophocles' Philoctetes* (New York: Farrar, Strauss and Giroux, 1961), 77.

8   Dante Alighieri, "The Inferno," *The Divine Comedy*, trans. Dorothy L. Sayers (New York: Basic Books), Canto 3, 1–5.

9   Charles Dickens, *A Tale of Two Cities* (Garden City, NY: Nelson Doubleday, 1999), 1.

Chapter 19

1   Khalil Ghibran, *The Treasured Writings of Kahlil Gibran,* trans. Anthony Ferris and Martin L. Wolf (USA: Castle Books, 1980), 51.

2   Adler, 452.

3   _____.

4   Tolstoy, "Kreutzer Sonata" as cited in Mike W. Martin's "Love's Constancy," *Philosophy* 68, no. 263 (January 1993): 63–77.

5   Edith Hamilton, "Orpheus and Eurydice," *Mythology* (Boston: Little, Brown and Company, 1942), 141.

6   Alan   Booth and David R. Johnson, "Declining Health and Marital Quality," *The Journal of Marriage and Family* 56, no. 1 (February 1994), 218.

7   K. A. S. Wicknama et. al., "Marital Quality and Physical Illness," *The Journal of Marriage and the Family* 59, no. 1 (February 1997), 143–55.

8   Christopher Lehman-Haupt, "Drawing Closer as She Slips Away," review of *Elegy for Iris* by John Bayley, "Books of the Times," *The New York Times* (December 24, 1998).

9   Mary Gordon, "Iris and John," review of *Elegy for Iris. The New York Times* (December 20, 1998).

10 _____.

11 Ed. Jeffrey Eugenides, *My Mistresses' Sparrow is Dead* (New York: HarperCollins, 2008), xvi.

12 _____.

Chapter 20

1   Shakespeare, *Hamlet*, I, ii, 129–37.

2   _____, 158.

3   Yeats, "The Second Coming," 189–90.

4   Jesse Rittenhouse, review of "Robert Frost, North of Boston," *The New York Times Book Review* (May 16, 1915).

5   Thomas Hardy, *Jude the Obscure* (New York: Harper and Row, 1966).

6   Michael J. Fox Foundation, general announcement via e-mail, March 3, 2010.

7   Thomas Hardy,   *The Works of Thomas Hardy in Prose and Verse* (London: The MacMillan Company Limited, 1912), 221.

Chapter 21

1   Shakespeare, "Sonnet 116."

2   Ralph Waldo Emerson, "Essays and English Traits," *The Harvard Classics*, ed. Charles W. Eliot (New York: P. F. Collier & Son Corporation, 1937), 112.

3   _____, 113.

4   Montaigne, "Of Friendship," 256–57.

5   _____, 247.

6   _____, 252.

7   Homer, *The Iliad*, book 18, ll, 24–28.

8   _____, 94–96.

9   Montaigne, 252.

10 _____, 106–10.

11 Homer, *The Iliad*, book 22, ll 389–97.

12 Genesis 2:20, 23–4.

13 Edmond Holmes, *The Triumph of Love* (London: John Lane, 1902), LI.

Chapter 22

1   Sontag, *Illness as Metaphor*, 3.

2   Virginia Woolf, *On Being Ill* (Amherst, MA: Paris Press, 2002), 8.

3   _____, *To the Lighthouse* (New York: Harcourt Brace and Company, 1990), 188.

4   _____, *On Being Ill*, 3.

5   Philip G. Hill, ed. *Our Dramatic Heritage* (Cranberry, NJ: Associated University Press, 1991), 80.

6   Sandblom, 22.

7   Sontag, 31.

8   _____, 28

9   Broyard, xiv.

10 Aimee Grutenberg, "If the Doctors are Right," *Journal of the American Medical Association* 273, no. 14 (April 12, 1995).

11 Sontag, *Illness as Metaphor*, 3–4.

12 _____, 21.

13 Aldous Huxley, *Words and Their Meanings* (Los Angeles: The Ward Ritchie Press, 1940), 8.

Chapter 23

1   Job, 28:12–28.

2   Anthony T. Kronman, *Education's End: Why Our Colleges and Universities Have Given Up on the Meaning of Life* (New Haven: Yale University Press, 2000), 85.

3   Alexander Pope, "Essay on Man: Epistle 2," *The Norton Anthology of English Literature, 2nd Edition*, vol. 2, ed. M. H. Abrams (New York: W. W. Norton & Company, 2000), 2,554.

4   Kronman, 240.

5   _____, 239.

6   Adler, 939.

7   Harold Bloom, *Where Shall Wisdom Be Found?* (New York: Riverhead Books, 2004), 3.

8   Adler, 939.

9   Walter Isaacson and Evan Thomas, *The Wise Men: Six Friends and the World They Made* (New York: Simon and Schuster, 1986).

10 John L. McKenzie, "Reflections on Wisdom," *Journal of Biblical Literature* 86 (March 1967), 1.

12 Jeremiah 8:22.

13 Herman Hesse, *Siddhartha* (New York: New Directions, 1951. 38.

14 Robert J. Sternberg, "What is Wisdom and How Can We Develop It?" *Annals of the American Academy of Political and Social Science* 591 (January 2004): 165.

15 "Baghavad Gita," *Harvard Classics* (New York: P. F. Collier and Son Corporation, 1969), Ch. XVI, ll, 1–17.

16   Robert Gordis, "Quotations in Wisdom Literature," *The Jewish Quarterly Review* 30, 123–24.

17   _____.

18   Shakespeare, *Hamlet*, III, i, ll, 75–82.

19   _____, III, i, ll, 164–65.

20   _____, I, ii, 130–34.

21   _____, III, iv, ll, 149–52; 56.

22   _____, III, i, 114–18;120; 128–29.

23   _____, II, ii, ll, 55; 575–76.

24   _____, III, iv, ll, 26–30.

25   Bloom, *Shakespeare: The Invention of the Human*, 3.

26   _____, *Hamlet: Poem Unlimited*, 139.

27   Bloom, *Where Shall Wisdom be Found*, 107.

28   Shakespeare, *Hamlet*, V, I, ll. 184-217.

29   Wordsworth, "Ode: Intimations of Immortality," vol. l, 59.

Chapter 24

1   Matthew 12:36–37.

2   J. Frank Dobie, "Words, Words, Words, My Lord," *The English Journal* 8, no. 1 (January 1919): 10.

3   Eds. Keith Ansell-Pearson and Duncan Large, "On Truth and Lies in a Nonmoral Sense," *The Neitszche Reader* (Malden, MA: Blackwell Publishing, 2006), 116.

4   Huxley, 9.

5   Edward Sapir, "The Status of Linguistics as a Science," *Language* 5, no. 4. (December 1929): 207–14.

6   George Orwell, *Nineteen Eighty-Four* (New York: Penguin Group, 1983), appendix.

Chapter 25

1   Alfred Lord Tennyson, "Locksley Hall," *The Norton Anthology*, 1,223; ll, 119–32.

2   Whitman, *Leaves of Grass*, vi.

3   Matthew 2:1–2.

4   Matthew 2:16.

5   Sophocles, 11–78.

6   Shakespeare, *Macbeth*, I, iii, ll, 50–51.

7   _____, IV, I, ll, 80; 92–94.

8   _____, V, viii, ll, 6–15.

9   Duncan J. Watts, "Is Justin Timberlake a Product of Cumulative Advantage?" *The New York Times*, (April 15, 2007).

10   Stevens, "The Poems of Our Climate," 315.

11 S. M. Fjellman, "Prescience and Power: God Emperor of Dune and the Intellectuals," *Science Fiction Studies* 13 (1986): 51–53.
12 Philip K. Dick, "Minority Report," *Selected Stories of Philip K. Dick* (New York: Pantheon Books, 2002): 227–64.

Epilogue

1   Percy Bysshe Shelley, "Hymn of Apollo," *The Complete Poems*, 651, vi, ll, 31–36.

Bibliography

Abrams, M. H., ed. *The Norton Anthology of English Literature*, 2nd edition, vol. 1, 2. New York: W. W. Norton & Company, 2000.

Adler, Mortimer J. "Happiness." *The Great Ideas: A Lexicon of Western Thought*. New York: Scribner Classics, 1992.

Alighieri, Dante. The Comedy of Dante Alighieri the Florentine. Translated by Lawrence Grant White. New York: Pantheon, 1948.

Ansell-Pearson, Keith, and Duncan Large, eds. "On Truth and Lies in a Nonmoral Sense." *The Neitszche Reader*. Malden, MA: Blackwell Publishing, 2006.

St. Augustine. *De Libero Arbitrio*, as cited in Payne, F. Anne. "Foreknowledge and Free Will: Three Theories in the Nun's Priest's Tale." *The Chaucer Review* 10, no. 3 (Winter 1976).

Baghavad Gita. *Harvard Classics*. New York: P.F. Collier and Son Corporation, 1969.

Barrett, William. *Irrational Man: A Study in Existential Philosophy*. Garden City, NY: Doubleday Anchor Books, 1958.

Bailey, Ronald. *Liberation Biology: The Scientific and Moral Case for the Biotech Revolution*. Amherst, NY: Prometheus Books, 2005.

Reason Magazine. August/Sept. 2002.

Beckett, Samuel. *Malone Dies*. New York: Grove Press, 1956.

Bellow, Saul. *Ravelstein*. New York: Viking, 2000.

Bellow. Saul. *Herzog*. New York: The Viking Press, 1964.

Blake, William. *The Complete Poetry and Prose of William Blake*. Edited by David V. Erdman. Los Angeles: University of California, Berkeley, 1982.

Bloom, Harold. *Genius: A Mosaic of One Hundred Exemplary Creative Minds*. New York: Warner Books, 2002.

Bloom, Harold. *Hamlet: Poem Unlimited*. New York: Riverhead Books, 2007.

Bloom, Harold., *Where Shall Wisdom be Found?* New York: Riverhead Books, 2004.

The Book of the Dead: The Hieroglyphic transcript and Translation into English of the Ancient Egyptian Papyrus of Ani. Commentary by E. A. Wallis Budge. New York: Gramercy Books, 1994.

Booth, Alan, and David R. Johnson. "Declining Health and Marital Quality." *The Journal of Marriage and Family* 56, no. 1 (February 1994).

Broyard, Anatole. *Intoxicated by My Illness*. New York: Ballantine Books, 1992.

Boswell, James. *The Life of Samuel Johnson*. New York: Alfred A. Knopf, 1992.

Campbell, Joseph (with Bill Moyers). Edited by Betty Sue Flowers. *The Power of Myth*. New York: Doubleday, 1988.

Camus, Albert. *The Stranger*. 1942. Translated by Matthew Ward. New York: Alfred A. Knopf, 1993.

Capek, Karel. *The Makropoulos Affair.*

Carroll, Lewis. *Alice's Adventures in Wonderland.* Norwalk, CT: Easton Press, 1977

Carver, Raymond. *Where Water Comes Together with Other Water.* New York: Random House, 1985.

Cavafy, C. V. *The Complete Poems of Cavafy.* Translated by Rae Dalven. New York: Harcourt, Brace & World, Inc., 1948.

Cervantes, Miguel de. *Don Quixote.* Translated by Edith Grossman. New York: HarperCollins Publishers, 2004.

Chodron, Pima. *When Things Fall Apart.* New York: Shambala, 1997.

Conrad. *Heart of Darkness.* 1902. New York: Alfred A. Knopf, 1993.

Conrad, Joseph. *Lord Jim.* 1900. Norwalk, CT: Easton Press, 1977.

Conrad, Joseph. *The Shadow Line. A Confession.* 1920. New York: Vintage Books, 2007.

Cunningham, Michael. *The Hours.* New York: Farrar, Strauss and Giroux, 1998.

Dante Alighieri. *The Comedy of Dante Alighieri the Florentine.* Trans. Dorothy L. Sayers. New York: Basic Books.

Dante's hell. http://padresteve.files.wordpress.com/2010/02/danteinferno_400x606.jpg.

Dick, Philip K. "Minority Report." *Selected Stories of Philip K. Dick.* New York: Pantheon Books, 2002.

Dickens, Charles. *A Tale of Two Cities.* Garden City, NY: Nelson Doubleday

Dickinson, Emily. *The Complete Poems of Emily Dickinson.* Edited by Thomas H. Johnson. Boston: Little, Brown and Company, 1960.

Dobie, J. Frank. "Words, Words, Words, My Lord." *The English Journal* 8, no. 1 (January 1919): 10.

Dostoevsky, Fyodor. *The Brothers Karamazov.* New York: Alfred A. Knopf, 1990.

Easterbrook, Gregg. *The Progress Paradox.* New York: Random House, 2003.

Edwards, Jonathan. "Sinners in the Hands of an Angry God." *American Sermons.* New York: The Library of America, 1999.

Eliot, T. S. *The Waste Land.* 1930. New York: Harcourt, Brace and Company, 1936.

Emerson, Ralph Waldo. "History." *Essays,* first series. 1841. New York: BiblioBazaar.

Emerson, Ralph Waldo. *Essays and English Traits.* The Harvard Classics edited by Charles W. Eliot. New York: P. F. Collier & Son Corporation. 1937.

Eugenides, Jeffrey, ed. *My Mistresses' Sparrow is Dead.* New York: HarperCollins, 2008.

Fitzgerald, F.Scott. *The Great Gatsby.* 1925. Shelton, CT: First Edition Library, 1953.

Fjellman, S. M. "Prescience and Power: God Emperor of Dune and the Intellectuals." *Science Fiction Studies* 13 (1986).

Frank, Edwin, ed. *Unkown Masterpieces.* New York: New York Review of Books, 2003.

Frost, Robert. From "Reluctance." 1913. *The Poetry of Robert Frost.* Edited by Edward Connery Latham. New York: Henry Holt and Company, 1969

Fukuyama, Francis. *Our Posthuman Future: Consequences of the Biotechnology Revolution.* New York: Picador, 2005.

The Gallup Organization. "Values and Beliefs Survey" as cited by Albert N. Winsman. *Commentary Magazine* (May 2004).

Ghibran, Khalil. *The Treasured Writings of Kahlil Gibran.* Translated by Anthony Ferris, Martin L. Wolf. USA: Castle Books, 1980.

Gomes, Peter J. *The Good Book: Reading the Bible with Mind and Heart.* New York, William Morrow and Company, Inc., 1996.

Gordis, Robert. "Quotations in Wisdom Literature." *The Jewish Quarterly Review* 30.

Gordon, Mary. "Iris ands John," review of *Elegy for Iris. The New York Times* (December 20, 1998).

Grutenberg, Aimee. "If the Doctors Are Right." *Journal of the American Medical Association* 273, no. 14 (April 12, 1995).

Gunersel, Adalet Baris. "Dionysian Frenzy—Myth or Reality?" *American Creativity Association Annual Conference* 2005.

Hamilton, Edith. "Orpheus and Eurydice." *Mythology.* Boston: Little, Brown and Company.

Hamilton, Edith, and Huntington Cairns, eds. *Plato: The Collected Dialogues.* Bolingen Series LXXI. Princeton: Princeton University Press, 1996. 4.

Hardy, Thomas. *Jude the Obscure.* 1895. New York: Harper and Row Publishers. 1966.

Hardy, Thomas. *The Works of Thomas Hardy in Prose and Verse*. London: The MacMillan Company Limited, 1912.

Hass, Robert, et. al., editors and advisory board. *American Poetry: The 20th Century. Vol. I*. New York: The Library of America, 2000.

Heaney, Seamus. *Beowulf. A New Version* Translation by Seamus Heaney. New York: Farrar, Strauss and Giroux, 2000.

Heaney. *The Cure at Troy: A Version of Sophocles' Philoctetes*. New York: Farrar, Strauss and Giroux, 1961.

Heaney. "What Passed at Colonus." *New York Review of Books* LL, no. 15 (October 7, 2004).

Hemingway, Ernest. *For Whom the Bell Tolls*. 1940. Shelton, CT: First Edition Library, 1968.

Hemingway. *The Nick Adams Stories*. New York: Scribner, 1972.

Hesse, Herman. *Siddhartha*. New York: New Directions, 1951.

Hill, Philip G., ed. *Our Dramatic Heritage*. Cranberry, NJ: Associated University Press, 1991.

Holy Bible: Old and New Testaments in the King James Version. Nashville: Thomas Nelson Publishers, 1978.

Holmes, Edmond. *The Triumph of Love*. London: John Lane, 1902.

Homer, *The Iliad*. Translated by Robert Fagles. New York: Viking, 1990.

Homer. *The Odyssey*. Translated by Robert Fagles. New York: Viking, 1996.

Hornblower, Simon, and Antony Spawforth, eds. *The Oxford Classical Dictionary*, 3rd edition. New York: Oxford University Press, 1996.

Huxley, Aldous. *Words and Their Meanings*. Los Angeles: The Ward Ritchie Press, 1940.

Isaacson, Walter, and Evan Thomas. *The Wise Men: Six Friends and the World They Made.* New York: Simon and Schuster, 1986.

Joyce, James. *A Portrait of the Artist as a Young Man*. 1916. Everyman's Library. New York: Alfred A. Knopf, 1991.

Joyce, James. *The Dubliners*. 1914. New York: Alfred A. Knopf, 1967.

Keats, John. "Endymion." *The Complete Poems of John Keats*. New York: The Modern Library, 1994.

Keats, John. *The Odes of John Keats*. Edited by Helen Vendler. Cambridge: The Belknap Press of Harvard University Press, 1983

Kristofferson, Kris. "The Pilgrim: Chapter 33." 1970. From *The Essential Kris Kristofferson*. SONY BMG, 2004.

Kronman, Anthony T. *Education's End: Why Our Colleges and Universities Have Given Up on the Meaning of Life*. New Haven: Yale University Press, 2000.

Kunitz, Stanley. *The Collected Poems*. New York: Norton.

Lattimore, Richmond, and David Greene, eds. *The Complete Greek Tragedies*, vol. 1 and 2. Chicago: University of Chicago Press, 1991.

Lawrence, D. H. "The Rocking Horse Winner." *The Oxford Book of Short Stories*. New York: Oxford University Press, 1981.

Lehman-Haupt, Christopher. "Drawing Closer as She Slips Away." Review of *Elegy for Iris* by John Bayley. "Books of the Times," *The New York Times* (December 24, 1998).

Lightman, Alan. *Einstein's Dreams*. New York: Pantheon Books, 1993.

Locke, John. "An Essay Concerning Human Understanding." Digitized Google e-book.

McCarthy, Cormac. *The Road*. New York: Alfred A. Knopf, 2006.

McKenzie, John L. "Reflections on Wisdom." *Journal of Biblical Literature* 86 (March 1967).

Marcus Aurelius. *Meditations*. Translated by Maxwell Staniforth. New York: Dorset Press, 1986.

Martin, Mike W. "Love's Constancy." *Philosophy* 68, no. 263 (January 1993).

Melville, Herman. *Moby Dick or The Whale*. 1852. Norwalk, CT: Easton Press, 1977.

Meninger, Karl. "The Academic Lecture on Hope." *The Journal of American Psychiatry* (December 1959).

Michael J. Fox Foundation. *General announcement*, March 3, 2010.

Milton, John. *Paradise Lost*. 1667. Norwalk: Easton Press, 1976.

Montaigne, Michel de. *The Essays of Michel de Montaigne*. Tanslated by George B. Ives. New York: The Heritage Press, 1946.

Moore, Thomas. *The Re-Enchantment of Everyday Life*. New York: HarperCollins Publishers, 1996.

Moriarty, Sheila, John Fasulo, Patricia Bissell, April Curfman, David Iverson, Petet Thompson, Pam Warford, Nancy Grandoff. Telephone interviews. December 2009–January 2010.

Nabakov, Vladimir. *Speak, Memory*. 1947. New York: Everyman's Library. Alfred A. Knopf.

Nabakov, Vladimir. "The Metamorphosis." *Lectures on Literature.* Edited by Fredson Bowers. San Diego: Harcourt, Inc., 1980. As transcribed online at http://victorian.fortunecity.com/vermeer/287/nabokov_s_metamorphosis.htm.

Orwell, George. *Nineteen Eighty-Four.* 1949. New York: Penguin Group, 1983.

Pope, Alexander. "Essay on Man: Epistle 2." *The Norton Anthology of English Literature, 2nd Edition*, vol. 2. M. H. Abrams, ed. New York: W. W. Norton & Company, 2000.

Rittenhouse, Jesse. "Review of Frost, Robert. *North of Boston.*" *The New York Times Book Review* (May 16, 1915).

Roose, Phyllis W. "The Poet's Heaven." *Gentlemen's Magazine* CCLXXXVI (June–September 1899).

Rose, Phyllis. *The Year of Reading Proust.* New York: Scribner's, 1997.

Rosen, Charles. "The Genius of Montaigne." *The New York Review of Books* (February 14, 2008).

Sandblom, Phillip. *Creativity and Disease.* London: Marion Boyars Publishers, 2009.

Sapir, Edward. "The Status of Linguistics as a Science." *Language* 5, no. 4. (December 1929). The Lingusitic Society of America.

Sartre, Jean-Paul. "The Flies." *No Exit and Three Other Plays.* 1946. New York: Alfred A. Knopf, 1976.

Seneca, Lucius. *On the Shortness of Life.* Translated by C. D. N. Costa. New York: Penguin Books, 1997.

Shakespeare, William. *The Riverside Shakespeare.* Boston: Houghton Mifflin Company, 1974.

Shelley, Percy Bysshe. *The Complete Poems of Percy Bysshe Shelley*. New York: Library of America, 1994.

Simpson, Harold B. *Audie Murphy: American Soldier*. Texas: Alcor Publishing Company, 1985.

Solzhenitsyn, Alexander. *The Cancer Ward*. New York: Farrar, Straus and Giroux, 1969.

Sondheim, Stephen. *Pacific Overtures*.

Sontag, Susan. "The Conscience of Words." *New York Review of Books* 25, September 1980.

Sontag, Susan. *Illness as Metaphor and AIDS and Its Metaphors*. New York, Farrar, Strauss and Giroux, 1990.

Sophocles. Oedipus the King. *The Complete Greek Tragedies*, The University of Chicago Press, 1959. Vol. II.

Sternberg, Robert J. "What is Wisdom and How Can We Develop It?" *Annals of the American Academy of Political and Social Science* 591. (January 2004).

Tennyson, Alfred Lord. "Locksley Hall." *The Norton Anthology.*

Tolstoy, Leo. *Anna Karenina*. Translated by Constance Garnett. Norwalk: Easton Press, 1975.

Watts, Alan. *The Way of Zen*. New York: Pantheon, 1989.

Watts, Duncan J. "Is Justin Timberlake a Product of Cumulative Advantage?" *The New York Times* (April 15, 2007).

West, Nathaniel. *Miss Lonelyhearts & The Day of the Locust*. New York: Modern Library Edition, 1998.

Whitman, Walt. *Leaves of Grass*. Facsimile of First Ed.: Brooklyn, NY, 1855.

Wicknama, K. A. S.; Frederick R. Lorenz, Rand D. Conger, and Glen H. Elder. "Marital Quality and Physical Illness." *The Journal of Marriage and the Family* 59, no. 1 (February 1997).

Wilde, Oscar. *The Short Stories of Oscar Wilde*. Norwalk: The Easton Press, 1976.

Woolf, Virginia. *Mrs. Dalloway*. 1925. New York: Alfred A. Knopf, Everyman's Library, 1993.

Woolf, Virginia. *The Common Reader*. 1925. First Series. London: Hogarth Press, 1962.

Woolf, Virginia. *On Being Ill*. 1930. Amherst, MA: Paris Press, 2002. 8.

Woolf. *To the Lighthouse*. 1927. New York: Harcourt Brace and Company, 1990.

Wordsworth, William. From "Ode: Intimations of Immortality on Recollections of Childhood." 1803–6. *The Complete Poetical Works of William Wordsworth*. Cambridge Edition. Edited by Andrew J. George. New York: Houghton Mifflin Company, 1904.

Wright, John W., ed. *The New York Times Guide to Essential Knowledge*. New York: St. Martin's Press, 2004.

Yeats, W. B. *The Complete Collected Works of W. B. Yeats: Volume I: The Poems*. Richard J. Finnerman, ed. New York: Scribner, 1983.

Zausner, Tobi. "When Walls Become Doorways." *Creativity Research Journal* (1998).

About the Author

Dean Scaros, Ph.D., is a native New Yorker whose professional career began as a teacher and college professor. He received his A.B. from Hunter College/CUNY, his M.A. in English from Teachers College, Columbia University and his PhD from New York University's Steinhardt School. After earning his doctorate Dean shifted focus from academia to business eventually rising to the position of president and chief operating officer of one of the nation's largest advertising agencies and later founded an agency of his own. Throughout his business life Dean remained devoted to the arts and literature and served as Visiting Clinical Assistant Professor of culture and communication at New York University.

After being diagnosed with Parkinson's, Dean turned to his first love – literature and art – which he found to be a source of inspiration and strength. He has two adult children and lives with his wife, Barbara, in Ridgefield, CT.

Made in the USA
Middletown, DE
14 May 2019